THE KINGDOM
OF
THE CRUSADERS

CHURCH OF THE HOLY SEPULCHRE,
DETAIL OF THE PORTAL

THE KINGDOM
OF THE CRUSADERS

by

DANA CARLETON MUNRO

*Late Dodge Professor of Medieval History
in Princeton University*

KENNIKAT PRESS, INC./PORT WASHINGTON, N. Y.

25435

PREFACE

FEW historians have known the period of the Crusades as thoroughly as did Dana C. Munro. This period was the subject of his special research throughout his active life. Hundreds of graduate students were initiated into historical research upon various phases of the Crusades in his seminar at the Universities of Pennsylvania and Wisconsin and at Princeton University. Many of these scholars continued their interest in this field and with his guidance and advice completed special studies for publication as articles, monographs, and books. His advice was sought also by others interested in this period of history. Few, if any, serious works on the Crusades or related problems were published in this country during the past generation which were not indebted to him for inspiration, guidance, or advice. This debt was partially recognized in the tribute paid him on his retirement from the presidency of the American Historical Association. On that occasion he was presented with the manuscript copy of *The Crusades and Other Historical Essays* by former students of his. A more complete record of this indebtedness must be sought in hundreds of studies which have been published in this country during the past forty years.

It was the hope of all interested in the period that

this extensive research might be crowned with a comprehensive work on the Crusades by the teacher and master of the field. There seemed every possibility that this hope and wish would be gratified, for he had definitely planned such a work and organized the accumulated materials so that he might devote all of his time to writing upon his retirement from active duties at Princeton. It was to be "his *magnum opus,* a detailed and scholarly history of the Crusades based on an exhaustive and critical use of the contemporary sources and vivified by a careful study on the ground of the regions traversed and occupied by the Crusaders. For the latter purpose he made a visit to the Near East." [1] This hope and plan were rudely shattered by his death on the very eve of his retirement from Princeton.

Fortunately, however, he had had occasion to organize a large part of his material in preparation for the Lowell Lectures at Harvard in 1924. In making his definite plans for the larger work during his last years at Princeton he was also revising these lectures for publication. The latter were thus much enriched by his plans for the larger work. The eight lectures had been devoted to the Latin Kingdom of Jerusalem involving the beginnings of the crusading movement and extending through the period of active possession of the Holy Land by the Crusaders. He had rounded out this theme by a discussion of the results of these activities and this intimate contact of West and East.

[1] E. P. Cheyney, article on D. C. Munro in *Dictionary of American Biography.*

As a result, in their revised form, these lectures afford a suggestive outline of the greater work. They contain his interpretation of the Crusades as a phase of the development of western Europe, as a phase in the relation of Europe and Asia, as a phase in the contact and mixture of race, culture, and civilization. They reflect the enrichment of the subject as a result of his journeys to the Near East and the modifications of his earlier conclusions, both from this source and from his latest researches in the field.

While enriched by revision in connection with the planning of the larger work on the Crusades, these lectures still retain the picturesque detail and colorful anecdotes of the original presentation. They will therefore appeal to the larger audience of general readers as well as to scholars in medieval history. It was probably in the interest of this larger audience that Munro followed the plan employed by A. Luchaire in his *Innocent III* of avoiding scholarly foot-notes. Quotations from the sources are incorporated in the text, the author of the quotation being mentioned as a rule. Scholars, familiar with the revised edition of Paetow's *Guide to the Study of Medieval History* will find in the sections on the Crusades and related topics in that work the key to the complete bibliography on this subject, for this bibliography was prepared under the author's own direction.

The revision of these lectures was nearly complete at the time of the author's death. The manuscript bore all the marks of the painstaking quest of verification which Cheyney has noted as characteristic of him. "From the beginning Munro insisted on the most rigorous scientific method. He laid down the rigorous rule that no statement must be made in historical writing for which a satisfactory reference to a contemporary source cannot be given." [2] The first six chapters had apparently undergone this careful verification almost to his complete satisfaction. Only a few queries on the margin indicated any intention of further verification. The last two chapters had not quite reached that stage. The indications of desired verification were more numerous, and in the last chapter there were variant versions of material as well as suggestions of points to be included. A detailed outline, however, afforded ample guidance for the completion of this chapter. It was possible to supply practically all of this material from his own writings. One paragraph on the mutual influence of Greeks and Latins required writing. Fortunately, directions in the outline indicated the nature of this paragraph. With this exception, editorial responsibility has been confined to the verification of points queried in the manuscript and the selection of the author's several statements to complete the last chapter. This work was done by the present writer, with the generous aid of Gertrude Doxey, Ph.D., State Teachers College, Bemidji, Minnesota.

Valuable aid and advice were received in the final preparation of the manuscript from Professor Philip

[2] E. P. Cheyney, *op. cit.*

K. Hitti, Walter L. Wright, and Shirley H. Webber
of Princeton University.

A complete bibliography of Munro's writings on
the Crusades has been added as an appendix.

A. C. KREY.

University of Minnesota.

CONTENTS

LIST OF MAPS AND ILLUSTRATIONS

MAPS

ILLUSTRATIONS

NOTES ON HEADPIECE AND TAILPIECES

The headpiece at the beginning of each chapter is a reproduction of the frieze over the west portal of the Church of the Holy Sepulchre in Jerusalem.

The tailpieces represent the following: page 29, a crusaders' coin in Arabic, struck at Acre in 1251 A.D. (note the crusading crosses); page 80, crusaders attacking a fortress (from a manuscript of William of Tyre); page 104, a ship of the thirteenth century (from William of Tyre); page 128, a coin of Tancred, nephew of Bohemond I and regent of Antioch; page 146, the seal of the Church of the Holy Sepulchre; page 173, a coin of Salah al-Din (Saladin); page 203, a party of crusaders returning from a foraging expedition (from William of Tyre).

The headpiece and the tailpiece on page 128 are reproduced from Archer and Kingsford, *The Crusades,* and the tailpieces on pages 80, 104, and 203 from Archer, *The Crusade of Richard I,* all by permission of the publishers, G. P. Putnam's Sons.

THE KINGDOM

OF

THE CRUSADERS

CHAPTER I

THE LAND AND THE PEOPLE

NORTH of Beirut where the Nahr al-Kalb, or Dog River, empties into the Mediterranean, the precipitous mountains of Lebanon come down to the very shore, leaving only a narrow pass. Through this invaders in all ages have been compelled to march. Thousands of years ago one conqueror had an inscription carved in the rock at the side of the path to record his achievements. Later other conquerors followed his example. At first there was only a trail well up on the mountain side which Nebuchadnezzar used; later a Roman road was cut out of the rock lower down by Marcus Aurelius; today an automobile road runs along the shore on which Allenby's troops marched. On one or the other of the three, within about a quarter of a mile, there are at least nineteen inscriptions, Egyptian, Babylonian, Assyrian, Chaldean, Greek, Roman, and so on through the ages, ending at present with those carved to commemorate the passage of the Allied troops in the Great War.

These inscriptions illustrate a fact of prime importance for the history of Syria: its central position between the great civilizations of the Nile Valley and the Euphrates, between the three continents, Asia,

Africa, and Europe, "in the luminous centre to which the rays emitted by the oldest civilizations, of Babylonia, Egypt, and Greece, converged." The inscriptions also illustrate the repeated conquests of Syria by foreigners.

And yet the road at Nahr al-Kalb, in spite of its record of so many invasions, is not as old and was not so much used in antiquity as the great caravan route from the Euphrates to the Nile which passed through Damascus, Galilee, the plain of Esdraelon, and the maritime plain to the coast road past Gaza, nor were the invaders who left their records at Dog River the only ones. The Hittites came down from the North and the Ethiopians came up from the South. Scythians ravaged the land. Persians, Parthians, Greeks, Romans, Arabs, and Turks had all in turn possessed Syria before the coming of the Crusaders; and Palestine had been held for a time by the Jews.

The inhabitants, whether subject to some conqueror or independent, were the natural intermediaries between the older civilizations and were greatly affected by their more powerful neighbors. Even today signs of the early Egyptian influence are clearly apparent; at Jubayl, the ancient Byblos, fragments of granite columns, brought from Assuan thousands of years ago to adorn the temples, lie scattered about the streets and are now used to roll the mud roofs of the houses. There, too, a few years ago M. Montet excavated an Egyptian temple of the twelfth dynasty and about the same time a landslip revealed an ancient sarcophagus with an inscription which may

Courtesy of Walter L. Wright, Jr.

ASSYRIAN AND EGYPTIAN INSCRIPTIONS AT NAHR AL-KALB

throw new light upon the early history of the alphabet.

This land has always been a religious center; temples and "high places" of worship are omnipresent in Syria and Palestine. Often the same site has been used for a succession of worships; Phoenician and Greco-Roman temples, unidentified shrines of older religions are interspersed among the sacred edifices erected by Jews, Christians, and Mohammedans. From time immemorial devotees have sought the River Adonis, the Grove of Daphne, Ba'labakk, Jerusalem, and countless other shrines; the land is a veritable museum of religions. At the present day adherents of strange cults are scattered among the many sects of Christians and Muslims.

The reason for their persistence in such close proximity is partly geographical. While Syria as a whole forms a unit, cut off from neighboring lands by mountains, desert, or sea, it is so divided internally that many spots are isolated. Rivers, which elsewhere form a means of communication, in Syria are barriers separating the peoples on the opposite banks. "In the whole country of Syria there is no river carrying boats except only for the ferry." Usually they are swift torrents flowing through deep gorges. Of the four large streams which spring from the Lebanon range, only two reach the sea—the Orontes, "the rebel," creator of Antioch, and the Litany which is of little importance; the Jordan, after forming two large lakes, ends in the Dead Sea; the Barada, to which Damascus owes its fertility and desirability, soon loses itself in the desert. At other places besides the mouth of the Dog River the mountains come down to the shore of the Mediterranean, isolating the neighboring seaports from one another. One of the best known instances is the Ladder of Tyre between that city and Acre. Consequently the land has always been divided into many small sections; the Tell el Amarna tablets of 3300 years ago show the same lack of unity which the Crusaders found; and the isolation is enhanced by the variations in climate and soil and the corresponding variation in animal and vegetable life.

Al-Muqaddasi, a tenth century Arab geographer, gave the classic description which has often been quoted: "Syria is very pleasantly situated. The country, physically, may be divided into four belts. The First Belt is that on the border of the Mediterranean Sea. It is the plain-country, the sandy tracts following one another, and alternating with the cultivated land. Of towns situated herein are Al-Ramlah, and also all the cities of the sea-coast. The Second Belt is the mountain-country, well wooded, and possessing many springs, with frequent villages, and cultivated fields. Of the cities that are situated in this part are: Bayt Jibril [Jibrin], Jerusalem, Nabulus [Neapolis], Al-Lajjun, Kabul, Qadas, the towns of the Bika [Biqa] district and Antakiyah [Antioch]. The Third Belt is that of the valleys of the Ghaur [Jordan], wherein are found many villages and streams, also palm trees, well cultivated fields, and indigo plantations. Among the towns in this part are Waylah, Tabuk, Sughar, Jericho, Baisan, Tiberias, Baniyas. The Fourth Belt is that bordering on the Desert. The mountains here are high and bleak, and the climate resembles that of the Waste; but it has many villages, with springs of water and forest trees. Of the towns therein are Ma'ab, 'Amman, Adhra'at, Damascus, Hims, Tadmur, and Aleppo."

"The climate of Syria is temperate, except in that portion which lies in the centre region of the province...."

"The coldest place in Syria is Ba'labakk and the country round; for among the sayings of the people it is related how, when men asked of the Cold, 'Where shall we find thee?' it was answered, 'In the Balqa;' and when they further said, 'But if we meet thee not there?' then the Cold added, 'Verily in Ba'labakk is my home.'

"Now Syria is a land of blessing, a country of cheapness, abounding in fruits, and peopled by holy men. The upper province, which is near the dominions of the Greeks, is rich in streams and crops, and the climate of it is cold. And the lower province is even more excellent, and it is pleasanter, by reason of the lusciousness of its fruits and in the great number of its palm trees."

The differences which Al-Muqaddasi notes are due in part to the two mountain ranges which run roughly parallel to the coast throughout much of the land and shut off Syria from the desert of Arabia. The difference in levels is very great; while the highest mountains rise about 9000 feet and have an Alpine flora, between the ranges lies a remarkable valley, or rather a series of valleys, of which the lowest point is the Dead Sea, about 1300 feet below the level of the Mediterranean. "This is the hot country where grow the indigo tree, the banana, and the palm."

These mountain ranges intercept the moisture-laden winds from the Mediterranean, and on their western slopes there were formerly extensive forests. The search for this lumber brought the first invaders from Egypt and Babylonia. Even in the time of the Crusades the thick undergrowth in the forest of Sharon impeded the forces of Richard the Lion-hearted. Today, except for the cedars of Lebanon and the pine forests at Beirut, most of the trees have disappeared, and any new growth is prevented by the goats and sheep.

There are only two seasons, the rainy and the dry. Beginning the latter part of October heavy showers pour down at intervals, "the former rains" of the Bible. During December, January, and February rains are constant. In March and the early part of April there are occasional heavy showers, "the latter rains" of the Bible. Hail storms are common and in the higher altitudes snow falls. Mt. Hermon is snow-capped, and on the Lebanon range the snow is some-times two feet or more deep; even in Jerusalem a snowfall is not infrequent. This rainy season inter-fered with the winter campaigns in the time of the Crusades, and fighting seldom began until late in May when the roads became passable. In the dry season showers are very rare, even rarer than in California, although the total annual rainfall in Jerusalem is about the same as in London.

In the spring after the rains the country is beautiful, and the sides of the mountains are frequently carpeted with flowers. It seems to be veritably a land flowing with milk and honey. Later, in the dry season, much of the interior is parched and barren, and the goats, who furnish the milk, are forced to eat every shrub, every pricking tree. Then the observer realizes that this is really a land of little more than milk and honey; that is, a semi-desert country which supported only goats and bees but which seemed good to the Children of Israel, seeking better pastures for their flocks. We must remember too that when Joshua sent out his spies to view the promised land (Joshua II) they crossed the Jordan and went to Jericho. The Jordan valley was long the garden of Palestine and Jericho was probably the most favored spot in the vicinity.

Eight hundred years ago the goats did little damage to the trees, partly because the land was more fertile, and partly because wild beasts were plentiful. Lions and leopards, hyenas and jackals, lurked in the forests where also bears and wild boars were found. Foxes, gazelles, herons, and cranes were plentiful, as they are today around Nabulus (Neapolis) in Samaria.

This land which was in parts so richly endowed and elsewhere semi-arid, with a configuration which isolated many districts, but situated on the highway between the ancient civilizations, contained a mixture

of peoples differing in race and religion. Since Syria
is the northern end of the peninsula of Arabia, most
of the population was Semitic, but, in the course of
ages, from the Semites had sprung many peoples
differing in language and religion, and non-Semitic
peoples had also found a home there. "Just as her
fauna and flora represent many geological ages, and
are related to the plants and animals of many other
lands, so varieties of the human race, culture, and
religion, the most extreme, preserve themselves side
by side on those different shelves and coigns of her
surface, in those different conditions of her climate.
Thus when history first lights up within Palestine,
what we see is a confused medley of clans—all that
crowd of Canaanites, Amorites, Perizzites, Hivites,
Girgashites, Hittites, sons of Anak and Zamzum-
mim." Early writers on the Crusades did not go far
astray when, in enumerating the inhabitants, they
cited all the names of eastern peoples with which
they were acquainted and then added the names of
various sects of heretics. In the thirteenth century
the pilgrim Burchard of Mount Sion says, "There
are dwelling therein men of every nation under
heaven, and each man follows his own rite." After
speaking of the Latins, Syrians, Saracens, and Greeks,
he adds, "There are also Armenians, Georgians, Nestorians, Nubians, Jacobites, Chaldeans, Medes, Persians, Ethiopians, Egyptians, and many other peoples
who are Christians." Most numerous of all were the
Syrians whom Burchard tells us "filled the whole
land," and Raymond of Agiles says there were at

least 60,000 in Lebanon. Cardinal Jacques de Vitry, who knew them well, says, "Since the days of old, they have dwelt in the land under divers lords, and borne the yoke of slavery successively under the Romans and Greeks, the Latins and barbarians, the Saracens and the Christians. These men are everywhere slaves, always tributaries, kept by their masters for husbandry and other ignoble uses; they are altogether unwarlike, and helpless as women in battle. ... They are for the most part untrustworthy, double-dealers, cunning foxes even as the Greeks, liars and turncoats, lovers of success, traitors, easily won over by bribes, men who say one thing and mean another, who think nothing of theft and robbery. For a small sum of money they become spies and tell the secrets of the Christians to the Saracens, among whom they are brought up, whose language they speak rather than any other, and whose crooked ways they for the most part imitate. They have mingled among the heathen, and learned their works; they shut up their wives after the Saracen fashion, and wrap up both them and their daughters with cloths, that they may not be seen. They do not shave their beards as do the Saracens, Greeks, and almost all Easterns, but cherish them with great care, and especially glory in them, holding the beard to be a sign of manhood, an honour to the face, and the dignity and glory of man. Like as eunuchs, who are quite beardless, are thought to be contemptible and effeminate by the Latins, so these think it to be the greatest disgrace not only to have their beards shorn, but to have a single hair pulled out of them.... The Syrians use the Saracen language in their common speech, and they use the Saracen script in deeds and business and all other writing, except for the Holy Scriptures, and other religious books, in which they use the Greek letters; wherefore in Divine service their laity, who only know the Saracenic tongue, do not understand them. ... The Syrians exactly follow the rules and customs of the Greeks in Divine service and other spiritual matters, and obey them as their superiors. As for the Latin prelates in whose dioceses they dwell, they obey them in word, but not in deed, and only in outward show say that they obey them, out of fear of their masters according to the flesh; for they have Greek bishops of their own, and would not fear excommunication or any other sentence from the Latins in the least, save that our laity would avoid all business or other dealings with them: for they say among themselves that all Latins are excommunicate, wherefore they cannot give sentence upon anyone."

Cardinal de Vitry was voicing the common feeling of the Franks about the Syrians, but we have reason to believe that he was not wholly just to them. The Crusaders sometimes employed them as soldiers, and on occasion they fought well; once a chronicler mentions their continuing a battle after the Franks had been forced to cease fighting on account of the heat. They had an excellent legal position, as will be noted later. They did not love the Franks,—why should they?—but threw in their lot with them because the Franks were successful. Most of them were engaged in agriculture or commerce, some were artisans, and a few scribes.

Closely connected racially with the Syrians but separated from them by religious dogmas and the language used in the church services, were the Maronites, inhabitants of the Lebanon. They were noted for their skill with the bow and were excellent fighters. Bishop William of Tyre praises their bravery and prowess, and even de Vitry excepts them from the general accusation of cowardice, which he brings against the other Christian natives. Although for a time they held a doctrine considered heretical, they joined the Roman Church in the twelfth century, but they have always retained their own patriarch.

Also dwelling in the Lebanon and elsewhere were Jacobites and Nestorians. In their case the line of division from the Syrians or the Maronites or from each other was theological. The Jacobites held that there was only one person in Christ, practised circumcision, and branded children before baptism. The Nestorians held that there were two distinct persons in Christ, and denied that Mary was the Mother of God. The Nestorians, the Jacobites, and the Maronites were the most highly educated of the native Christians, and were noted for their skill in architecture, and the Jacobites were especially esteemed for their medical knowledge. They were much respected by the Franks and were favored in their legislation. The Nestorians and the Jacobites were at first the chief intermediaries from whom the Franks acquired some of the oriental civilization.

There were many Greeks in Syria. They belonged to the Orthodox Church which had two patriarchates, one in Jerusalem and the other at Antioch, and many wealthy monasteries. They were regarded by the Franks as unwarlike and treacherous, as is shown in de Vitry's description of the Syrians. Because of the hostility that developed between the Greek emperors and the Crusaders, the Greeks were much less esteemed than the Syrians, and did not have as good a legal position, although some of the later kings married Greek princesses.

The Armenians formed a considerable element of the population in the north. Some time before the Franks entered the country Armenian chieftains had established themselves in the mountain fastnesses of Cilicia, where they were threatened both by the Greek emperor, who claimed the whole country, and also by the Turkish conquerors. They accordingly welcomed the Crusaders, believing that they had come, as Matthew of Edessa says, "to break their chains and free them from the infidels." The Armenians were good fighters and were a great aid to the first Crusaders, especially in constructing military engines. They were keen merchants or peddlers, dealing with both Muslims and Christians. They were frequently denounced for their treachery. They used their own language, the Armenian, and had their national church. They were far less advanced in civilization than the Syrians or the Saracens, and conse-quently, as will be noted later, eagerly borrowed the usages of the western invaders, with whom they mingled and intermarried freely.

Only one other Christian sect was numerous enough to require mention here,—the Georgians. Those that lived in Syria were noted either for their bravery or piety, and some were given especial praise for their warlike qualities. There were a number of Georgian monasteries, one of which, near Antioch, contained sixty monks. Some of the monks still imitated St. Simeon Stylites and were known as pillar saints. They used the Greek language and were affiliated with the Greek Church, but not obedient to its officials, as they had a bishop of their own.

All of these native Christians were divided from one another by their religious dogmas and seldom intermarried, but they were necessarily tolerant of one another and had learned to live together under foreign masters without too much friction. It is scarcely necessary to add that all were heretics from the western standpoint.

There was a considerable number of Jews and Samaritans. The Jews were especially well versed in the art of dyeing, and almost every town had one or more Jewish masters of this trade. It is impossible to say how many were living in Palestine or Syria at the beginning of the Crusades—probably more than later under Frankish rule, when there may have been some 2500 in the territory held by the Christians. The Samaritans kept themselves rigidly apart from the Jews. They were extremely intolerant. One of the earlier pilgrims tells how the Samaritans followed them about carefully and burnt away with straw all traces of their footprints. They were too keen traders to refuse to sell to the Christians, but this same pilgrim records that the pilgrims had to throw their money into a vessel of water so that it might be cleansed from defilement before the Samaritans would touch it. There were also slaves from almost all nations and of many creeds.

All of these peoples were subject to the Muslims. In the last half century before the coming of the Franks the Seljukian Turks had overrun Asia Minor and the northern part of Syria. After the death of their leader, Malek-Shah, they had divided into many separate bands, all mutually hostile, each seeking only its own advantage. The total number of the Turks was comparatively small, as they were only a military caste dominating the cities that they held; it is especially noteworthy that these leaders rapidly took on the civilization of their subject peoples.

The great mass of Muslims were Arabs or Saracens, but as in the case of the Christians there were representatives of many peoples, and they were divided by differences in religious beliefs and practices. In addition to the two great divisions of Shi'ites and Sunnites, there were many religious sects among the Muslims, including some who may have worshipped idols, and many other sects whom the Christians usually, although incorrectly, classed with the Muslims, such as the Druzes and Yezidi or devil worshippers.

Some of the Saracens were dwellers in towns, merchants and artisans, as a class on a much higher plane of civilization than the Franks. Others were agriculturalists, farming the land for their lords, under conditions which were probably more onerous than those of the serfs in western Europe. Then too there were the Bedouin, living in their black tents, leading their herds from one pasture to another, just as they did in the days of Abraham, just as they do today, of whom Doughty has drawn an inimitable picture. They were contemned by the others as "eaters of snakes, lizards and jerboas." Some Bedouin occasionally settled down and became farmers when they found a favorable opportunity.[1]

The central position and religious importance of Syria fostered the growth of cities. Earthquakes, conquests, and misrule have destroyed most of the older ones; the Hittite city of Kadesh was almost entirely buried under the lake of the same name. The Phoenician 'Amrit still awakens our wonder by the extent of its ruins, although for at least two millenniums it has been used as a quarry and plundered for building material by the people of the neighborhood. Other Phoenician cities have prolonged their existence, even to the present day, with many changes of masters.

Damascus, "the gateway of the desert," may be the oldest city in Syria, and possibly the oldest city in the world which has had a continuous existence. Its foundation is ascribed to Uz, the great-grandson of Noah. "The early history of Damascus is shrouded in the mists of a hoary antiquity. Leave the matters writ-

[1] When Syria had lost much of its population after the Great War, it was most interesting to see instances of Bedouin taking up the vacant lands and gradually becoming settled on the soil.

ten of in the first eleven chapters of the Old Testament out, and no recorded event has occurred in the world but Damascus was in existence to receive the news of it. Go back as far as you will into the vague past, there was always a Damascus.... To Damascus years are only moments, decades are only flitting trifles of time. She measures time not by days, months, and years, but by the empires she has seen rise and prosper and crumble to ruin. She is a type of immortality. She saw the foundations of Ba'albec [Ba'labakk], and Thebes, and Ephesus laid. She saw these villages grow into mighty cities and amaze the world with their grandeur, and she has lived to see them desolate, deserted, and given over to the owls and bats. She saw the Israelitish Empire exalted, and she saw it annihilated. She saw Greece rise and flourish two thousand years, and die. In her old age she saw Rome built, she saw it overshadow the world with its power; she saw it perish. The few hundreds of years of Genoese and Venetian splendour and might were to grave old Damascus only a trifling scintillation hardly worth remembering. Damascus has seen all that ever occurred upon earth, and still she lives. She has looked upon the dry bones of a thousand empires, and will see the tombs of a thousand more before she dies. Though another claims the name, old Damascus is by right the Eternal City."

This may be somewhat exaggerated, but "not only can no city lay claim to such high antiquity, but few can vie with it in the importance of the events which have happened within its walls. Twice it has been the capital of great emperors. At one time its monarch ruled from the shores of the Atlantic to the Himalayas and the banks of the Indus.... Her riches must have been royally splendid until Tamerlane, whom the citizens still call 'Al-Wahsh,' the wild beast, in 1401 ordered a hideous massacre.... The writings of the fathers of the Eastern Church, antiquities, manuscripts, silk divans ornamented with gold and jewels, rich fabrics, libraries filled with rare literature, Arabesqued walls and ceilings, palaces with marble halls and inlaid fountains, all disappeared under the horse-hoofs of 'Al-Wahsh.' "

Damascus had gained this wealth partly by trade, partly by its own industries. From Damascus started the most important pilgrimage to Mecca each year, and consequently thither came from all parts of the world Muslims to participate in this pilgrimage. Wares from the Far East and Persia were brought thither by caravans to be exchanged for the products of Arabia and Egypt. Its citizens were noted for their manufacture of silk, of gold brocade, of weapons, of sweets—Damascus sweets which are still renowned. The city was only three days' journey distant from Beirut and four from Tyre and Acre. The advantages of commercial intercourse were recognized very early by the Crusaders, and Godfrey made a "firm peace with Damascus on account of trade."

When the Franks first entered Syria, Antioch was its most important city. Compared with Damascus, Antioch was new, but it had already an age of 1400 years. Situated twenty miles from the sea, on the bank of the Orontes, in the midst of a fertile plain, its mighty walls enclosed a space of some four square miles. Under the Antonines it had been the third city in the Roman Empire, and the most important in the Greek East. Although the Saracens conquered and held it for over three centuries, it had been recovered by the Byzantine Empire in 968 and remained a Greek city until a few years before the First Crusade. It was noted for its manufactures and schools, its beautiful churches, splendid houses, and gardens. Silk vestments woven at Antioch were highly prized by the ecclesiastics in the West, as is shown by the inventories of treasures at Canterbury and at St. Paul's, London. The glass vessels made at Antioch also had a far-extended fame. Soap was an important manufacture, as it still is, and the Franks soon learned from their contact with the natives the convenience of using it. The education, especially in medicine, was far superior to that in the West and continued to flourish under the rule of the Crusaders; later, Theodore of Antioch became the physician of Emperor Frederick II. There was an abundant supply of water; and many of the water pipes are still in position on the now barren mountain sides within the old city walls. Gardens and fountains adorned the houses of the more substantial citizens, who had preserved from antiquity their delight in bathing.

Damascus and Antioch were the chief cities, but there were many other centers of industry and refinement: in the northeast, Aleppo, Hims, and Hamah, which were never conquered by the Crusad-

ers; on the coast a long line of ports,—Laodicea, noted
for its luxury; Tortosa, famed for its camel-hair
stuffs; Tripolis, with its medical school; Beirut, formerly a great law center; the old Phoenician towns of
Tyre and Sidon, which with Acre were important
entrepôts of commerce; Caesarea, which Herod had
made into a magnificent city, and where he erected
sumptuous palaces and an amphitheater; Ascalon,
"the bride of Syria"; and many others less well
known. In the interior were Jerusalem, the goal of
pilgrims, Jewish, Christian, and Muslim; Jericho in
its wonderful setting; Neapolis, the Sichem of the
Bible, called by the Muslims "the little Damascus";
Tiberias on the beautiful Sea of Galilee; Nazareth,
Bethlehem, and many another spot familiar to every
reader of the Bible. The cities in the north were more
important and prosperous than those in Palestine
because the goods brought by caravan from China
and Asia found their outlet to the Mediterranean
mainly through Damascus, Aleppo, Antioch, Tripolis, and the intervening or neighboring cities.

There was an active trade with many parts of Asia.
Both the Arabs and the Chinese had merchant vessels which traversed the Indian Ocean and the Persian Gulf. Silks, spices, and other articles of luxury
were brought from China and the spice islands. A
vivid glimpse of the commerce of the time, which
recalls the voyages of Sindbad the Sailor, is given by
a contemporary. In Kish he talked with a merchant
who told him that he planned only one more venture
before retiring to enjoy his wealth, much as Sindbad

did after his voyages. He planned to take a cargo of sulphur from Persia to China, where it was in great demand and sold at a high price. Then he would take Chinese porcelain to Greece, Greek brocade to India, Indian steel to Aleppo, glass from Aleppo to Yemen, and finally striped goods to Persia. Such was the common method of carrying on trade at that time. Bagdad was the center of all this transcontinental trade, and thence it flowed westward to the great emporiums of Islam, Aleppo, Damascus, Antioch, Tripolis, and other centers.

In addition to the manufactures previously noted, the cities also produced rugs, camelot, silk and cotton fabrics, beer, sugar, salt, iron and glass ware, damascene, copper, pottery, and porcelain. The oldest part of the bazaar at Jerusalem and the underground bazaar at Tripolis which are still preserved give us some idea of the habits of trade, and the spice bazaar at Jerusalem is redolent of the same far eastern products which were brought in such great quantities to Syria before and during the time of the Crusades.

Naturally these commercial cities had to have a food supply, and each was surrounded by farms and villages. The land was kept productive by extensive systems of irrigation. At Hamah the great wheels which raise the water from the Orontes still charm the inhabitants with the music of their wailing so that the leading citizens feel it incumbent upon them to celebrate the water-wheels in verse. Other remains of the irrigation system survive here and there, but the land of Syria today is barren compared with its fertility when the Crusaders first entered it. They were amazed by sugar cane, oranges, figs, dates, apples of paradise (bananas), melons, grapes, olives, and balm of Gilead. Most of the grains cultivated today, except Indian corn, were then grown more profusely. Agriculture seems to have been carried on intelligently with a systematic rotation of crops. The results may be judged from the enthusiastic account which Al-Muqaddasi gives. "Unequalled is this Land of Syria for its dried figs, its common olive oil, its white bread, and the Ramlah veils; also for the quinces, the pine-nuts called 'Quraysh-Bite,' the 'Aynuni and Duri raisins, the Theriack antidote, the herb of Mint, and the rosaries of Jerusalem. And further, know that within the Province of Palestine may be found gathered together six-and-thirty products that are not found thus united in any other land. Of these the first seven are found in Palestine alone; the following seven are very rare in other countries; and the remaining two-and-twenty, though only found thus all together in this province, are, for the most part, found one and another singly, in other countries. Now the first seven are the pine-nuts called 'Quraysh-Bite,' the Quince or Cydonian-apple, the 'Aynuni and the Duri raisins, the Kafuri plum, the fig called Al-Saba'i, and the fig of Damascus. The next seven are the Colocasia or Water Lily, the Sycamore, the Carob or St. John's Bread [Locust-Tree], the Lotus-fruit or Jujube, the Artichoke, the Sugar-cane, and the Syrian apple. And the remaining twenty-two are the fresh dates and olives, the shaddock, the indigo and juniper, the orange, the mandrake, the Nabk fruit, the nut, the almond, the asparagus, the banana, the sumach, the cabbage, the truffle, the lupin, and the early prune, called 'Al-Tari'; also snow, buffalo-milk, the honey-comb, the 'Asimi grape and the Tamri- [or date-] fig. Further, there is the preserve called Kubbayt; you find in truth the like of it in name elsewhere, but of a different flavour. The Lettuce also, which every-where else, except only at Ahwaz [in Persia], is counted as a common vegetable, is here a choice dish."

As a further summary of both the manufacturing and the agricultural products may be quoted the ac-count by the same Al-Muqaddassi of the commerce in Syria. "From Palestine come olives, dried figs, raisins, the carob-fruit, stuffs of mixed silk and cotton, soap and kerchiefs. From Jerusalem come cheeses, cot-ton, the celebrated raisins of the species known as 'Aynuni and Duri, excellent apples, bananas—which same is a fruit of the form of a cucumber, but the skin peels off and the interior is not unlike the water-melon only finer flavoured and more luscious,—also pine-nuts of the kind called 'Quraysh-Bite,' and its equal is not found elsewhere; further—mirrors, lamp-jars, and needles. From Jericho is brought excellent indigo. From Sughar and Baisan come both indigo and dates, also the treacle called 'Dibs.' From 'Am-man, grain, lambs, and honey. From Tiberias, carpet stuffs, paper, and cloth. From Qadas, clothes of the stuff called 'Munayyir' and 'Bal'isiyah' and ropes. From Tyre come sugar, glass beads and glass vessels both cut and blown. From Ma'ab, almond kernels. From Baisan, rice. From Damascus come all these: olive oil, fresh pressed, the 'Bal'isiyah' cloth, brocade, oil of violets of an inferior quality, brass vessels, paper, nuts, dried figs and raisins. From Aleppo, cotton, clothes, dried figs, dried herbs and the red chalk called 'Al Maghrah.' Ba'labakk produces the sweetmeat of dried figs called Malban."

In such a favored land the Saracens had inherited a highly developed civilization from the period of the Greek and Roman domination and had brought thither as a result of their conquest of so much of the known world both learning and products gathered from India, Persia, Egypt, and other lands. While Syria in the eleventh century was not one of the great centers of Muslim learning, it was far in advance of the west of Europe, and the Franks were exposed to a liberal education in their contact with the natives. Leaders among these natives were frequently of a character to inspire the respect and admiration of the Franks who came to know them.

We are fortunate in having a so-called autobiography of one of the leaders, Usamah, who was born on the 4th of July in the same year as the Council of Clermont, 1095, and died a pensioner of Saladin the year after the latter captured Jerusalem. Usamah called his book "Learning by Example," and in his old age he set down the things that seemed to him noteworthy in his long experience. Incidentally, he tells us much of his father's life as well as of his own. From it we can reconstruct in broad outlines the life led by an educated Arab-Syrian gentleman at the time when the Crusaders first settled in the Holy Land.

Usamah's family had risen to prominence only a short time before the First Crusade. In 1081 his grandfather had obtained possession of Shayzar on the Orontes. This was a very strong castle already famous in the days of Mohammed. The river surrounds on three sides the base of the cliff, or "the cock's crest," on which Shayzar stands. The position is almost impregnable by nature and was fortified with great skill. The only entrance was by a bridge across the Orontes, which could easily be defended, and then by a passage cut in the rock. The grandfather died only a year after the stronghold had been granted to him for his services. He was regarded with great veneration by Usamah, who resembled him in many respects. Both were warriors and poets, and Usamah, almost one hundred years after the death of his grandfather, delighted in repeating the verses which the latter had composed. Under Usamah's family Shayzar became the resort of poets and learned men.

An uncle of Usamah succeeded to the lordship of Shayzar and added to its possessions by conquest. The country immediately surrounding it was fertile and supported possibly 5000 warriors, very different from today when only a few hundred fellahin draw from it a scanty existence. The castle is still a magnificent ruin, comparatively untouched by the earthquakes which have destroyed so many others. The uncle died

CASTLE OF SHAYZAR, HOME OF USAMAH, FROM SOUTHWEST

CASTLE OF SHAYZAR FROM SOUTHEAST, SHOWING ORONTES
RIVER

when Usamah was three years old, leaving the inheritance to Usamah's father, but the latter declined the
lordship because he detested the task of ruling and the
endless diplomacy or chicanery which seemed essential to the preservation of one's position in the
troubled state of Syria. He exclaimed, "I shall not,
by Allah, accept the lordship, as I would rather make
my exit from this world in the same condition as I
made my entrance into it." The lordship went to a
younger brother, and Usamah's father devoted his
life to pious pursuits and hunting, when he was not
obliged to fight. He was very brave and his body
bore many scars of terrible wounds. By predilection,
he "employed all his time reading the Koran, fasting
and hunting during the day, and copying the Book
of Allah (exalted is he!) at night. . . . He was wont
to ride for the hunt one day and rest the next day
and fast incessantly." "Despite his heavy body and
advanced years, my father (may Allah's mercy rest
upon his soul!), who was always fasting, would gal-
lop all day long, and he would never go hunting except on a fine hunter or a fleet pack horse, and would
feel neither weak, worn out nor tired; although we,
his four children, while with him, would feel fatigued
and exhausted." He was noted for his skill in callig-
raphy, an art in which he had perfected himself while
he was on an embassy in Persia, and he made forty-six
complete copies of the Koran. For each he composed
a different conclusion, some of them replete with
learning. He seems to have given away three during
his lifetime. The other copies he wished to have

buried with him, and he designated four of the most magnificent on which he wished his head to repose.

As he was especially fond of hunting, he collected dogs, falcons, and other birds of prey from Persia and Constantinople, as well as all Syria. He was especially successful in training the falcon. He organized hunting parties as a general prepared for a battle. He kept up this recreation even until his old age so that he retained his health and joy in living. The father was also a poet, and one of his poems which has been preserved and translated into French shows originality and ingenuity. He was skilled in astrology and wished to educate Usamah into its mysteries, but the latter took little interest in it. He was the soul of honor, and ready to sacrifice all to keep his word. On one occasion he charged Usamah to lay down his life if necessary to rescue some Frankish and Armenian hostages who had been released by him but afterward captured by another Muslim chief. "Pursue the ambuscade with thy men, hurl yourselves on them and deliver your hostages."

The women of the family were worthy of the men and highly respected by Usamah. Their position in the household was one of great honor, and Usamah contemns the Franks' attitude toward their wives because it was so different from that in his own circle. On occasion the Saracen women could fight bravely and encourage their men to combat. Their advice was often sought and followed. Once when the rulers were away, some Isma'ilites (Assassins) seized Shayzar by treachery. Usamah's grandmother and mother organized the defense so that all the Isma'ilites were finally put to death "on the day after the strife." Brought up by such a father and mother, Usamah developed into a brave and learned gentleman. He studied at Tripolis for nearly ten years under the direction of the head of the school of science. All his life long he was intimately associated with the Crusaders and formed friendships with some of the Franks. His anecdotes, some of which will be quoted later, illustrate the relations between the natives and the Crusaders and the opportunity the latter enjoyed for gaining new impressions and knowledge.

CHAPTER II

THE CONQUEST OF THE LAND

In 1095 western Europe was in turmoil. The investiture struggle was dragging on between the emperor and the pope, and Germany and northern Italy were torn by civil war. The pope, Urban II, was a fugitive from Rome, which was held by an anti-pope. The king of France, ruling over only a small territory, was surrounded by powerful lords who were independent or semi-independent of his authority, and he himself was excommunicate. In England, which was still suffering from the effects of the Norman conquest, William Rufus was oppressing the people by his tyranny. Everywhere in western Europe private warfare was common, in spite of the efforts of the Church to check it through the Peace of God and the Truce of God. France was over-populated, and many of the fighting men, especially Normans, had left it to seek their fortunes elsewhere, in England, in Italy, or still farther afield. Reports of their success excited others to dissatisfaction with their condition at home and made them ready for new adventures.

Many of the more pious, oppressed by the feeling that the times were out of joint, were turning to religion. Early in the century the people had begun eagerly to vie with one another in building new churches. "It seemed as though the world were throwing off its decrepitude to clothe itself anew in an array of white sanctuaries." New and stricter monastic orders were being founded and were filled with enthusiastic recruits. Others sought outlet for their religious feelings by going on pilgrimages to the sacred shrines scattered throughout Europe and the Near East, of which Jerusalem was the most important. For centuries this had been the goal of many an earnest soul led by the pious wish to worship "where His feet have stood." Others had gone to expiate their crimes, for the journey to Jerusalem was the extreme penance imposed for the most heinous crimes such as incest, parricide, or the burning of a church. The movement was greatly accelerated in the eleventh century; while the number of pilgrimages to Jerusalem recorded for the preceding centuries was six in the eighth, twelve in the ninth, sixteen in the tenth, there are said to have been one hundred and seventeen separate expeditions during the eleventh century before the beginning of the Crusades, and some of these expeditions had included large numbers, even thousands, of pilgrims.

As we survey the last quarter of the eleventh century, we realize the restlessness of the peoples everywhere in western Europe. This restlessness showed itself in various forms; it was manifested chiefly in warfare and in asceticism, but in the cities, and especially those in maritime Italy, it expressed itself in increased concern with commercial ventures.

In the East, the Byzantine Empire, seemingly crushed by the defeat of the emperor by the Seljukian Turks at the battle of Manzikert in 1071, had shown its "marvelous vitality and power of recuperation." Under Alexius Comnenus the empire had been strengthened; the attack of the Normans, Robert Guiscard and his son Bohemond, had been beaten off; the Petchenegs had been conquered; but the Turks had not been driven back. The latter had overrun most of Anatolia and Syria, which Alexius wished to reconquer. For this task the depleted forces of the empire were insufficient, so that he was obliged to turn for aid, as so often before, to the West. At the Council of Piacenza in March, 1095, his envoys were present to beg help from the assembled nobles, lay and ecclesiastical.

Urban II was a statesman and grasped the opportunity. He was anxious to heal the schism between the Greek and the Latin Churches which had been separating them for forty years. He saw the possibility of checking private warfare in the West and uniting all Christendom under his own leadership. As he considered the matter after the Council of Piacenza, his plans grew in magnitude. A call for aid for Constantinople would bring some volunteers, but to accomplish his purpose a greater incentive was necessary. Between March and November his plans were matured, and in the latter month he held a great Council at Clermont in Auvergne for which he had made careful preparations. He had sounded out some of the prospective leaders and gained their support, especially that of his vassal, Count Raymond of Toulouse, the most powerful lord in the south of France. The success of his appeal at Clermont shows how well he understood his age and how carefully formed had been his plans.

On November 27, 1095, in the open fields, because no building could hold the throng, Urban preached the First Crusade. He dwelt upon the sufferings of their fellow Christians in the East and the pollution of the sacred places by the heathen. He depicted the evil conditions at home because of warfare and poverty. He urged his hearers to go to the relief of their brethren and to free the Holy City from the infidel; to acquire merit by fighting righteous wars instead of imperiling their souls by fighting at home; to march under the leadership of Christ, with the assurance that if they died they would gain an eternal reward, if they lived they would possess the Holy Land flowing with milk and honey. "Many orations have been delivered with as much eloquence and in as fiery words as the Pope used, but no other oration has been able to boast of as wonderful results." The incentives were those that appealed to the dominant characteristics of the western peoples: piety, love of adventure, love of fighting, eagerness to better their lot. Small wonder that those present joined in the shout "It is the will of God," which had been determined upon as the battle cry, and pressed forward to take the cross. The enthusiasm was so great that even the aged and infirm, monks and women and children, were among those demanding to receive the sacred emblem. Urban tried in vain to dam the current. His eloquence had aroused the emotions of the multitude and had determined the character of the expedition. It was to be composed of a nucleus of armed men, real fighters, but the great mass was made up of non-combatants, women, and children, utterly unfit to fight for the cause of the Crusade.

Many of the latter were impatient to set off at once without waiting for the date set by the pope. They found their leader in Peter the Hermit. It is not known whether he was at the Council of Clermont or not, but soon after the proclamation of the Crusade there, he was preaching at the crossroads and in the towns, stirring many by his eloquence. An abbot, Guibert of Nogent, who may have heard him preach, has left a description of him which shows his wonderful influence and success. "He was from the city of Amiens, if I am not mistaken, and we learned that he had lived as a hermit in the garb of a monk somewhere in northern Gaul, I know not where. We beheld him leaving there, with what intent I do not know, and going about through cities and towns under the pretext of preaching. He was surrounded by such great throngs, received such enormous gifts, and was lauded with such fame for holiness that I do not remember anyone to have been held in like honor. He was very generous to the poor from the wealth that had been given him. He reclaimed prostitutes and provided them with husbands, not without dowry from him; and everywhere with an amazing authority, he restored peace and concord in place of strife. Whatever he did or said was regarded as little short of divine, to such an extent that hairs were snatched from his mule as relics. This we ascribe not so much to the popular love for truth as for novelty. He wore a plain woolen shirt with a hood and over this a cloak without sleeves, both extending to his ankles, and his feet were bare. He lived on wine and fish: he hardly ever, or never, ate bread...."

As Peter went from place to place he was followed by an enthusiastic throng composed mainly of peasants but including some knights. The peasants were not all poor, for Guibert tells us that some set out with their possessions and their children in carts drawn by oxen. Their ignorance was so great that, as they approached a town, the children would ask eagerly if it was Jerusalem. Peter's march led him through central France into the Rhine valley. At Cologne he stopped for a time to preach. Some of his followers, impatient to be on their way to the Holy Land, left at once under the conduct of an able knight, Walter the Penniless, and set out for Constantinople. They were followed two weeks later by Peter and the remainder of the host. On the whole their march was successful. It is eloquent of the good order which they maintained that their progress as far as Hungary was entirely without opposition and that the armies which followed them found no hostile feeling but instead were joined by many volunteers. When they reached Constantinople Peter and his followers were impatient to cross the Hellespont, and the emperor, who found them troublesome guests—it is said that some stole the lead off the roof of churches to sell it for old junk—had them conveyed over to Asia Minor. There they soon perished at the hands of the Turks, only a remnant, including Peter, escaping.

Other bands excited by the news of Peter's march gathered under various leaders. These began their expedition to the Holy Land by plundering the Jews in the cities along the line of march, and by their excesses provoked such hostility that almost all were exterminated.

In the meantime nobles in various parts of western Europe had been preparing for the long journey. About the chief leaders gathered the great hosts. Those from Lower Lorraine followed their duke, Godfrey of Bouillon, who was brave, religious, honest, a leader beloved by his men. With him went his brother Baldwin who was destined to become the first king of Jerusalem. We are especially well informed about his march and deeds because in the host which followed him was a knight who wrote an account of the expedition which was afterwards incorporated in one of the histories of the Crusade. Godfrey and his host marched along the so-called road of Charles the Great, the same which Walter the Penniless and Peter the Hermit had followed, down the Danube valley and across to Constantinople.

The contingent from the Ile de France followed Hugh the Great, brother of the king. The latter, because he was excommunicate, took no part in the

movement, but he urged his vassals to take the cross
and designated his brother as their leader. Hugh, tall,
handsome, and vain, was surrounded by a body-guard
of handsome knights in shining armor, but he had
few of the qualities of a great commander, and played
only an insignificant part in the Crusade. He went to
Italy and crossed to Greece, where he was taken in
charge by a representative of the emperor and conducted to Constantinople.

The most powerful among the leaders was Count
Raymond, ruler of Toulouse, whose forces were so
large that, with the customary exaggeration of the
age, he is said to have led 100,000 men. He
is well described by a contemporary, "as fanatical
as a monk, as land greedy as a Norman." With him
went Adhemar, bishop of Puy, whom Urban II had
designated as his legate to go with the Crusaders.
This was a happy choice. His character, his skill as a
military chief, his tact in overcoming friction between
the other leaders, his lack of fanaticism, made him an
ideal representative of the pope. Raymond's chaplain, also named Raymond, wrote a very full account
of the Crusade and has left a record which is precious,
partly because he was thoroughly honest, but especially because he was imbued with the religious, cre-
dulity of the age and depicts the miracles and visions
which were so frequent. He tells of the march almost
due eastward to Constantinople.

The ablest of all the leaders was Bohemond, son of
Robert Guiscard. The father had built up a strong
duchy in southern Italy and had attempted the con-

quest of the Eastern Empire, in which he had been ably seconded by Bohemond. Before his death he designated as his heir Roger, a younger brother, and Bohemond was left almost without property. Some he acquired by successful warfare, but he eagerly seized upon the Crusade as an opportunity to carve out a principality for himself in the East. He was followed by many Normans from southern Italy, including his kinsman, Tancred. The latter, the hero of Tasso's *Jerusalem Delivered,* was brave and unscrupulous, very different from the ideal character depicted in later literature. Bohemond crossed to Durazzo and marched through the Greek Empire to Constantinople. Among his followers was an anonymous knight who kept a kind of diary of the expedition which is the most important source for the First Crusade. With some additions it forms the anonymous *Gesta Francorum,* which was so often copied by the writers of a slightly later date.

Among the other leaders only the two Roberts and Count Stephen can be mentioned here. Robert, Count of Flanders, whose father had made a pilgrimage to Jerusalem and had been in correspondence with Emperor Alexius, went to Italy and thence proceeded without any especial difficulty to Constantinople. Duke Robert of Normandy with his customary impetuosity mortgaged his duchy to his brother, King William of England, and the latter is said to have collected from the duchy in the first year twice as much as he paid for the whole term of years. Count Stephen

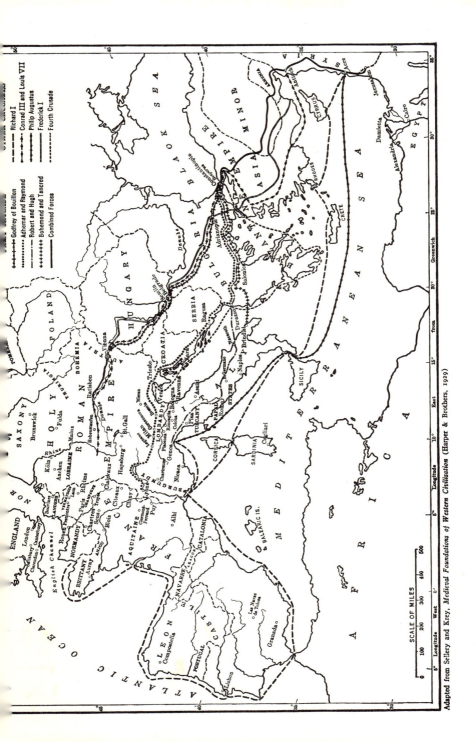

Adapted from Sellery and Krey, *Medieval Foundations of Western Civilisation* (Harper & Brothers, 1929)

of Blois, son-in-law of the Conqueror, was one of the wealthiest of the participants, and is said to have had three hundred and sixty-five castles, one for each day in the year. The two Roberts and Stephen had come to Italy together, and in their company went Fulcher of Chartres, who wrote a chronicle which is very valuable because of the naïveté with which he recounted events.

The choice of different routes by the leaders indicates careful planning and correspondence among them. It was fortunate that in 1095 both the land and sea routes were open; the former had been made possible by the conversion of the Hungarians to Christianity early in the century; the latter, by the expulsion of the Muslims from Sicily in 1091. The date set by Urban for the beginning of the expedition was August 15, 1096. This date was probably chosen in order to give ample time for preparation and to make certain that the year would be far enough advanced to assure plenty of fodder and supplies along the way. It is also highly probable that he had hoped that the Crusaders would be able to march through Asia Minor and Syria in the cooler part of the year. Unfortunately, the leaders were late in starting and there were many delays along the way and especially in Constantinople, so that they actually arrived in Asia Minor in the extreme heat of summer.

It is impossible to make an estimate of the total number who participated in the movement. In the different hosts there were men from all parts of west-

ern Europe, even from the uttermost isles of the sea.[1]
Fulcher says, "But who ever heard such a mixture of
languages in one army? There were Franks, Flemish,
Frisians, Gauls, Allobroges, Lotharingians, Alemanni,
Bavarians, Normans, Angles, Scots, Aquitanians,
Italians, Dacians, Apulians, Iberians, Bretons, Greeks
and Armenians." William of Malmesbury, who generally follows Fulcher rather closely, here adds, "the
Welshman left his hunting; the Scot his fellowship
with lice; the Dane his drinking party; the Norwegian
his raw fish." There was scarcely a village which was
unaffected by the movement. One writer attempted
to reckon the approximate number in the host by the
length of time it took them to cross a bridge over a
certain river in Asia Minor, and his estimate has
been taken seriously by some other writers. There are
only three objections to his conclusion: first, the size
of the bridge is not known; second, the length of the
time it took the Crusaders to cross the bridge is not
known; third, it is not certain—it is in fact improbable
—that they crossed this bridge. Anna Comnena, the
daughter of Emperor Alexius, says that the Crusaders
were innumerable, like the leaves on the trees and
the stars in the sky.

At first there was a general feeling of brotherhood,
of participation in a common cause. Some Crusaders
who were unable to talk any language understood by
the others made the sign of the cross with their fingers
and were joyfully welcomed. "But though we spoke

[1] A generation ago one enthusiastic writer identified the unknown
isles of the sea as the eastern coast of North America and told of
contingents who went on the Crusade from our own land.

diverse languages, we were, however, brothers in the
love of God and seemed to be nearest kin. For if one
lost any of his possessions, whoever found it kept it
carefully a long time, until, by inquiry, he found the
loser and returned it to him."

As they went on their way the people intermingled.
As they saw new towns and strange sights they had
much to talk about and acquired new ideas. The
process can be traced dimly in the pages of the chronicles and in the letters sent home by the chiefs. Especially were they moved by the sight of the great
city of Constantinople. There was nothing like it in
the West. Its wealth, its great buildings, its countless
convents, the many relics in the churches, and the
beauty of its women most impressed the rude Westerners.

Naturally, at first, the relations between the Greeks
and the Crusaders were strained. Alexius was alarmed
at the size of the enormous hordes which were pouring into his lands. Although the different armies of
the Crusaders had on the whole preserved good order
and done little damage in their march to Constantinople, there had been occasional conflicts with the
emperor's troops; more than one town had been
sacked; and one of the bands was led by his old
enemy, Bohemond. On the other hand the Crusaders
were suspicious of the Greeks and had a great contempt for them. The two were in very different stages
of civilization, and the feeling of a common religion
which might have united them against the infidel had
been sorely strained by the schism since 1054.

Both parties were anxious to work together. The Crusaders felt the need of the emperor's aid and supplies on their march to Jerusalem, and the emperor was desirous of reconquering his territories which had been overrun by the Turks. Yet, because of the mutual contempt and suspicions, misunderstandings were inevitable. The emperor was determined to force all the leaders to take an oath to respect his rights and to restore to his empire any conquests they might make, but the leaders were very loath to give up their independence and to become his vassals. After much friction and some fighting one leader after another was induced to take the oath which the emperor desired. Raymond of Toulouse and Tancred were the most obdurate. Raymond finally consented to take a modified form of the oath. Tancred evaded it temporarily by crossing into Asia Minor.

The oath was the oath of fealty common in the West, which the emperor had borrowed for the occasion, but it was complicated by the Byzantine custom of "filiation," which to the emperor implied a much closer subordination. For example we read that "Godfrey acknowledged himself not only as his son, according to the custom of the country, but also with clasped hands as his vassal." Yet the leaders did not intend to become merely mercenary troops under the emperor. The compact which was drawn up and sworn to by both parties laid duties upon each; and if either party did not fulfill the obligations the other party would, theoretically at least, be freed from all his obligations. The suspicions engendered in the negotiations about taking the oath and the nature of the compact were certain to result in friction and in mutual charges of bad faith.

An event which occurred at the time of the formal ceremony when the leaders took the oath has often been related and was used in *Count Robert of Paris* by Sir Walter Scott. Anna Comnena, the emperor's daughter, describes it thus: "Thus they all assembled, Godfrey amongst them, and after the oath had been taken by all the Counts, a certain venturesome noble sat down on the Emperor's seat. The Emperor put up with him and said not a word, knowing of old the Latins' haughty nature. But Count Balduinus stepped forward and taking him by the hand raised him up, rebuked him severely, and said, 'It was wrong of you to do such a thing here, and that too when you have promised fealty to the Emperor; for it is not customary for the Roman Emperors to allow their subjects to sit beside them on the throne, and those who become his majesty's sworn bondmen must observe the customs of the country.' He made no reply to Balduinus, but darted a fierce glance at the Emperor and muttered some words to himself in his own language, saying, 'Look at this rustic that keeps his seat, while such valiant captains are standing round him.' The movement of the Latin's lips did not escape the Emperor, who called one of the interpreters of the Latin tongue and asked the purport of his words. When he heard what the remark was, he said nothing to the Latin for some time, but kept the saying in his heart. As they were all taking leave of the Emperor, he called that haughty-minded, audacious Latin, and enquired who he was and of what country and lineage. 'I am a Frank of the purest nobility,' he replied, 'all that I know is that at the cross-roads in the country whence I come there stands an old sanctuary, to which everyone who desires to fight in single combat goes ready accoutred for single combat, and there prays to God for help while he waits in expectation of the man who will dare to fight him. At those cross-roads I too have often tarried, waiting and longing for an antagonist; but never has one appeared who dared to fight me.' In reply to this the Emperor said, 'If you did not find a fight when you sought for it then, now the time has come which will give you your fill of fighting. But I strongly advise you not to place yourself in the rear nor in the front of your line, but to stand in the centre of the "hemilochitae," for I have had a long experience of the Turkish method of fighting.'" The scene is eloquent of the emperor's difficulties and of the great difference in customs and manners which separated the new allies.

At first they worked together and all besieged Nicæa, where the first œcumenical council had been held in 325 A.D. The siege lasted for over seven weeks. The crude machines of war which were constructed at first were soon destroyed by the enemy. Finally a Lombard engineer built a more effective one, and by the aid of this a tower was undermined. This is interesting as an example of the way in which the Crusaders from the different lands acquired from one another the skill for which each was noted. On one side of the city is a large lake by means of which the besieged received provisions and aid. Finally boats were dragged overland from the Bosporus and launched in the lake. Then the inhabitants realized the hopelessness of further resistance and surrendered to the emperor. The Crusaders had been anticipating eagerly the joys of sacking the city, the plunder in valuables and women which would be theirs. But the emperor did not permit the Crusaders to do any plundering or even to enter the city except in small bands. To assuage their feelings of disappointment the emperor made great gifts to the leaders, so that Stephen of Blois wrote home to his wife that he had received more than he got in her dowry. Among the common people some measures of brass coins were distributed, which was so unsatisfactory to them that one chronicler wrote that "the Emperor Alexius showed such gratitude to the army that they will always curse him and proclaim him a traitor."

From this time the misunderstandings and resentments increased. Although the leaders, won by the emperor's gifts, renewed their oaths to him—at this time Tancred also was obliged to take the oath—yet there was little further common action. The Crusaders set out on their long march to Jerusalem, accompanied by only a small Greek force which was so unimportant that it is not mentioned as taking any part in the battles. The emperor remained behind with his troops to profit by the terror occasioned by the Crusaders' army, which enabled him to recapture many towns and to extend the boundaries of his power. Gibbon says, "In a style less grave than that of history, I should perhaps compare the Emperor Alexius to the jackal who is said to follow the steps, and to devour the leavings, of the lion." Undoubtedly the emperor's policy was a shrewd one, but not one which would bind the crusading chiefs more closely to him.

Nicæa had been captured on June 19, 1097. Stephen of Blois, who had been chosen as chief of the whole expedition, in the same letter in which he wrote about the great amount of money he had received, said, "We shall be in Jerusalem in five weeks unless Antioch resists us." The five weeks were to be extended to more than two years, and the crusading hosts were to encounter many dangers and losses before they reached the Holy City. Because of the difficulty of conducting so great a host along one road, the leaders separated, and on July first one division was surprised near Dorylaeum by a huge army of Turks and Arabs. "The Turks crept up, howling loudly and shooting a shower of arrows. Stunned, and almost dead, and with many wounded, we immediately fled. And it was no wonder, for such warfare was new to us all." This division of the Crusaders would have been destroyed if aid had not come opportunely from the warriors in the other division who turned defeat into victory so that the Turks were repulsed with great slaughter. This victory was very important for the Crusaders, for it freed them from danger of any further attack by the Turks in Asia

Minor, who were too demoralized by their defeat to raise another army.

As the Turks and Arabs fled before the Franks, they devastated the country in order to impede the advance of the Crusaders. The latter suffered terribly from the lack of food and water and from the heat. It was July, and their march, as one chronicler says, "was through deserts and dry and uninhabitable land from which we scarcely escaped and came out alive. Hunger and thirst parched us on all sides, and there was absolutely nothing for us to eat, unless, by chance, tearing and grinding grain with our hands, we continued to exist on such food as wretchedly as possible. There most of our cavalry ceased to exist because (thereafter) many of these became foot-soldiers. For want of horses many of our men used oxen in place of cavalry horses, and because of the very great need, goats, sheep, and dogs served as beasts of burden." And another chronicler, in describing the same march, says: "Truly one could not know whether to laugh or to cry from pity when many of our men loaded sheep, goats, hogs, and dogs with their supplies.... The skin of these animals was worn by the weight of the baggage. And knights with their armor sometimes even mounted oxen." Pregnant women gave birth to premature babies who were abandoned along the way. The falcons which the nobles had taken with them died. When the army reached a river they drank to such excess that many perished.

Finally they came to lands which had not been

devastated by the Turks and where water was more plentiful. Some of the chiefs left the main host in order to make conquests for themselves. Tancred and Baldwin quarreled and fought over the possession of Tarsus in Cilicia which each one claimed by right of conquest. It fell eventually to the Normans as Baldwin, tempted by an invitation from the Armenian ruler of Edessa, went thither accompanied by eighty knights. There he succeeded in obtaining possession of the city and founded the first state established by the Crusaders in the Orient. His English wife who had accompanied him on the Crusade had died in Asia Minor, and he was therefore able to strengthen his position by marrying an Armenian princess. This was the first of many such marriages between the crusading nobles and Armenians.

About the twenty-first of October the main army camped before Antioch. After their long march and great suffering they were glad to rest in such an attractive spot. "We found there every abundance— vines full everywhere, pits full of grain, trees bent down with fruit, and many other goods useful for the body." The abundant food was soon squandered, as the Crusaders "did not care to eat anything except the thighs and the shoulders of cattle, and only a few were willing to eat the breast." Then a new period of suffering followed, as they were harassed by the Turks when they went beyond the confines of the Christian camp in their search for food, and the horses were dying for lack of fodder. "Now grain and all food began to be excessively dear before the birthday of the Lord. We did not dare to go outside; we could find absolutely nothing to eat within the land of the Christians, and no one dared to enter the land of the Saracens without a great army.... And so the poor began to leave, and many rich who feared poverty. If any for love of valor remained in camp, they suffered their horses to waste away by daily hunger. Indeed, straw did not abound; and fodder was so dear that seven or eight solidi were not sufficient to buy one night's food for a horse." The Armenians and Syrians from the city brought some food for which they charged exorbitant prices. Many Crusaders were so discouraged that they fled; Peter the Hermit attempted to, but was caught and brought back. Just after Christmas a great earthquake added to their terror; "though in this way God chastised his army... yet the minds of some were so blind and abandoned that they were recalled neither from luxury nor robbery." Bishop Adhemar "prescribed a fast of three days and urged upon the people prayers and alms-giving, together with a procession; moreover, he commanded the priests to devote themselves to masses and prayers; the monks to psalms. Thereupon the merciful Lord, remembering His compassion, put off the punishment of His children, lest the arrogance of their adversaries increase."

In the midst of these troubles Taticius, the Greek commander who had been sent by the emperor to accompany the Crusaders with a small force of Greeks, left, giving as an excuse that he was going to procure re-enforcements and provisions. The siege dragged on, and it was reported that a great Turkish army was advancing to the relief of the city. Under these circumstances all the leaders except Raymond agreed, unless Emperor Alexius came to their aid, to hand over the city to Bohemond, if he could capture it. He had already suborned one of the officers of the garrison, who early in the morning of June 3, 1098, let down a rope ladder. Bohemond and his men climbed to the tower, opened one of the gates, and the city was captured after the siege had lasted over seven months.

Enormous riches were found in Antioch. While the Crusaders were "engaged in counting and identifying their spoils and had desisted from the siege of the citadel, and listening to the pagan dancing girls feasted in splendor and magnificence, not at all mindful of God who had granted them so great a blessing, they were besieged by the pagans on the third day." Well might the commander of the Muslims boast that he had the Franks shut up in Antioch, while he held the citadel above the city; that he had them in the hollow of his hand and would put them all to death or else lead them away into slavery.

Some of the Crusaders fled from the city. Many who remained were forced by starvation to eat their horses and asses. "Most of the knights lived on the blood of their horses; awaiting the mercy of God, they did not yet want to kill them." Leaves of trees, grape vines, and thistles were cooked to allay their hunger. This lasted for twenty-six days. Stephen of Blois, who had been chosen in Asia Minor as chief of the whole expedition, ran away; he and the others who let themselves down from the walls by ropes were contemptuously styled "rope-dancers." Stephen hastened north and met Emperor Alexius advancing with an army which included some Crusaders. He was coming to take possession of the cities which had been conquered, but when he learned from Stephen's account of the desperate plight of the Crusaders he left them to their fate and ordered a retreat. Stephen went with him and returned to the West.

As Stephen of Blois had fled and Count Raymond, the bitter enemy of Bohemond, was ill, the Christians, shut up in Antioch, chose Bohemond as their leader. In the midst of their panic, while they were on the verge of despair, many were enheartened by what they believed to be a direct interposition of God's mercy. Peter Bartholomew, a peasant, told Bishop Adhemar and Count Raymond that he had had a vision, before the capture of the city, in which St. Andrew appeared to him, conducted him into Antioch, and showed him the Holy Lance with which the side of the Saviour had been pierced as He hung upon the cross. This lance was buried in the Church of St. Peter. The bishop did not believe the man's story, but Count Raymond did. He with his chaplain and ten others accompanied the peasant to the church and there they dug in vain from morning till evening; finally the peasant who had had the vision descended into the hole and brought forth the lance. Many rejoiced in the miracle, but others were sceptical; in particular, Arnulf, chaplain of the count of

Normandy, ridiculed the vision. But as the sufferings and starvation increased the leaders decided to make use of the lance and ordered a fast of three days, a procession, a general confession, and then an attack upon the enemy. Bishop Adhemar led Count Raymond's men, and his division carried the lance. The Muslims were surprised and after a sharp battle were routed. Now that the lance had served its purpose and the Crusaders were safe no one of the leaders venerated it or believed it genuine except Raymond.

Between him and Bohemond there was bitter strife, because Bohemond claimed Antioch in accordance with the promise made to him by the other leaders. Raymond insisted that it should be handed over to Emperor Alexius because of the oath which the other leaders had taken, and he refused to give up to Bohemond the towers in Antioch which his troops held. In spite of Alexius' not coming to their aid when they were in dire straits the other leaders were unwilling to take any action which might seem to be in violation of their agreement with the emperor, and although they were favorable to Bohemond's claim they were not disposed to commit themselves. Unfortunately the only man who might have reconciled the various factions, the papal legate, Adhemar of Puy, died soon after the victory which saved the Christians. He was mourned by all, and the chiefs wrote to the pope urging him to come in person to lead the host, now that his legate was dead.

The strife between the leaders became more bitter. "For each one thought only of his own advantage," to quote one of the chroniclers, "no one cared for the common good." Before obtaining Antioch the Crusaders had captured one hundred and sixty-five towns and fortresses in Syria, and garrisons had been left to guard these. Baldwin had obtained Edessa and its territory, and many a landless man had become lord of a city. As the other knights were anxious to secure possessions and spoils, the advance to Jerusalem was postponed from time to time. But the poorer people in the army became impatient and proposed to choose "some brave knight," who would lead them to Jerusalem, and Godfrey of Bouillon encouraged them as he was anxious to go on. This spirit of revolt among the people led Bohemond and Raymond to make a "discordant peace," as a chronicler calls it. Raymond set out followed by many. But Bohemond remained behind and soon expelled from Antioch the garrison which Raymond had left to guard his possessions, and thus obtained the whole city.

Raymond started in January, 1099, and was soon joined by the other leaders, except Baldwin and Bohemond, but there was no unity. Arnulf, a priest, secure in the support of some, openly ridiculed the lance, and criticism became so acrimonious that the peasant who found the lance had to offer to undergo an ordeal to prove its genuineness. Two fires made of dry olive branches covering a space thirteen feet long and four feet high and only a foot apart, were kindled so that they burned fiercely and the flames shot up thirty cubits high into the air. Then Peter Bartholomew, clothed only in his tunic, carrying the lance, entered the fire. When he emerged, according to those who believed in the lance, he was unharmed, but was wounded by people in the crowd who threw themselves upon him and trampled on him in their desire to touch him or to get a piece of his garment as a relic; by the hostile faction it was believed that he had been condemned by God. However he may have been wounded, he died in a few days, and the lance was still a subject of controversy; it was the symbol of the hostility between the different factions.

At first they marched up the valley of the Orontes as far as Shayzar, then they turned westward to the plain of Tripolis and marched down along the coast. The rulers of the cities attempted no opposition. The commander in Tripolis freed slaves, sent presents and food, and promised to consider surrender after the capture of Jerusalem; the ruler of Beirut did the same. The march was facilitated by the terror inspired by victories of the Crusaders over the two armies, the dissensions among the Muslims, the unwarlike attitude of the majority of the population accustomed to submit to any conqueror, and the attitude of the caliph of Egypt, who, profiting by the Seljuks' preoccupation in the north, had taken Jerusalem from them in 1098. There was even talk of an alliance between him and the Crusaders against the Seljuks.

But the mass of the crusading host was intent upon the capture of Jerusalem. After many delays, for they did not leave Beirut until May 20th, the army finally arrived before the Holy City on June 7th. Of the leaders there were present Raymond, Godfrey, Robert of Flanders, Robert the Norman, and Tancred. On the advice of a hermit who lived on the Mount of Olives, they made one attack which was fruitless because they had no scaling ladders. They had little food and were obliged to bring water from a distance of six miles, as the Saracens had filled up the springs and destroyed the cisterns in the neighborhood of the city. Moreover the Saracens lay in wait for them when they went out to get the water and slaughtered many. The Crusaders were disheartened and neglected to build siege machines. Finally, incited by the clergy, they determined to seek God's aid and to make preparations for the assault; humbly, with bare feet, led by the clergy, all made a procession around the walls of Jerusalem. While they marched outside, "the Saracens and Turks made the circuit on the walls," ridiculing the pilgrims and mocking the cross. In addition the Crusaders built siege machines, for which the necessary timbers had to be brought from a long distance. Then they prepared for the attack by prayer, fasting, and alms-giving. As the assault was made with desperate bravery and the city was defended with equal valor, the result was uncertain for two days and a half. One of the chroniclers estimated the number of the Christians able to bear arms at not more than 12,000 and the number of the defenders at 60,000. Finally on July 15th the Crusaders captured the city.

Then followed an indiscriminate slaughter which

spared neither age nor sex. "Piles of heads, hands, and feet were to be seen in the streets of the city. It was necessary to pick one's way over the bodies of men and horses." The leaders wrote exultantly to the pope, "If you wish to know what was done with the enemy who were found there know that in Solomon's porch and in his temple our men rode in the blood of the Saracens, up to the knees of their horses."[2] The following day some three hundred Saracens who had taken refuge on the roof of the Temple were found and killed, but that ended the slaughter. On the next day, that is two days after the capture, the leaders "ordered all the Saracen dead to be cast outside because of the great stench, since the whole city was filled with their corpses; and so the living Saracens dragged the dead before the exits of the gates and arranged them in heaps, as if they were horses. No one ever saw or heard of such slaughter of pagan people, for funeral pyres were formed from them like pyramids, and no one knows their number except God alone."

When we contrast with this the conduct of Saladin when he captured Jerusalem from the Christians in 1187, we have a striking illustration of the difference between the two civilizations and realize what the Christians might learn from contact with the Saracens in the Holy Land.

[2] According to Lane-Poole, they massacred 70,000. *History of Egypt,* VI, 164.

CHAPTER III

ESTABLISHMENT OF THE KINGDOM

THE Crusade had been successful. On July 15, 1099, after a siege of over five weeks, Jerusalem had been captured. The next step was to provide for the government of the Holy City. Even before its capture the leaders had held a council to consider the election of a ruler. For, during the three years that they had been on the march to Jerusalem, there had been no definite head to the movement. As long as he lived, Bishop Adhemar of Puy, the papal legate, had exercised a considerable, although indefinite, authority. He had been able to do so partly because of his position as the representative of the pope, Urban II, but mainly because of his ability and tact. A contemporary chronicler described him as—

> Gracilis ad equitandum
> Et facilis ad omne bonum.

On horseback he had shown himself well fitted to lead a division of the army, as he had done in the battle at Antioch against Kerbogha. By his tact he had prevented the enmities which existed among the chiefs from wrecking the expedition. After his death at Antioch, on August 1, 1098, the leaders had written to Urban begging him to come in person to lead the movement which he had started. The pope, not able to do this, had appointed Dagobert, archbishop of Pisa, as his legate. The latter, however, did not arrive at Laodicea before the end of August, 1099, and the Crusaders at Jerusalem had no knowledge of his appointment until after his arrival in Syria.

After the capture of Antioch, in spite of the previous agreement, there had been bitter strife as to who should hold the city. To prevent such a contingency after the taking of Jerusalem, the leaders, as already stated, had held a council to discuss the matter. But members of the clergy had objected to the selection of a lay head for the Holy City. They said that no king ought to rule where our Lord suffered and was crowned. They suggested that some layman should be made "advocate," or defender, of Jerusalem. This title was chosen by the clergy, because it was a common custom in the West for some lay lord to be "advocate" of a monastery. No agreement was reached, and the leaders postponed action.

Two days after the capture of the city another council was held. The clergy urged that a spiritual head should first be chosen, but the leaders were determined to elect a lay ruler. Their choice fell upon Raymond, count of Toulouse. He refused the honor, saying, it is reported, that he would be horrified to bear the title of king of that city, but that he would consent to the election of someone else if anyone would accept it. This caused a delay of several days. It is reported that the crown was offered to other leaders, especially to Robert of Normandy. If so, they all refused. Finally a week after the capture of the city Godfrey was chosen, but he was not made king and he did not wear a crown. His title was "Defender [Advocate] of the Church of the Holy Sepulchre." He was still most commonly called "Duke" from his position in the West as duke of Lower Lorraine. His official style was "Godefridus dux gratia Dei ecclesiæ S. Sepulcri nunc advocatus."

The clergy had apparently won a victory. Jerusalem was to be an ecclesiastical city, not the center of a feudal state. Their victory is emphasized by the position of Godfrey's name in the superscription to the letter written to the pope from Laodicea in September, 1099, where the bishops are given precedence over Godfrey; for it was the general rule in the Middle Ages that in letters the names of those who were of superior should precede those of lesser rank.

Any conflict between the lay and ecclesiastical powers in Jerusalem was averted temporarily by the election of Arnulf of Rohes to the chief position of the church. He was a learned clerk who had been tutor to one of the daughters of William the Conqueror. According to his opponents, he was a man of low morals whose amours had made him a by-word throughout the army. This is probably not true, as he had been chosen to preach the sermon on the Mount of Olives before the capture of Jerusalem. He had been the leader in proclaiming the fraud of the Holy Lance at Antioch, and consequently was the object of hatred to its partisans. Of more importance for his later fortunes was the fact that he was the son of a priest, and therefore technically ineligible to hold a church office. He was the most important leader among the clergy, and was chosen while Raymond and his followers had gone on a pilgrimage to the Jordan. He was bitterly hated by Raymond, and consequently was obliged to look to Godfrey for support. The two worked together during the few months when Arnulf was head of the church in Jerusalem. There is some doubt as to his exact title. Probably he was elected patriarch, but as it was in the absence of Raymond and the Provençals, he was chosen by only a part of the army. His election was never ratified by any superior ecclesiastical power, and consequently later he was spoken of as "quasi-patriarch."

Union was necessary at this time. Less than a month after the election of Godfrey, the Crusaders learned that the sultan of Egypt was advancing with an enormous army to recapture Jerusalem and annihilate the Christians. The peril was so imminent that all the Christian forces in Palestine joined together to avert the blow. Only the aged and infirm were left at Jerusalem, under the care of Peter the Hermit, to pray for the success of their defenders. The two armies met near the city of Ascalon. The Christian leaders reported, later, to the pope that their army numbered only 5,000 horsemen and 15,000 foot-soldiers, while "there were probably in the enemy's army 100,000 horsemen and 400,000 foot-soldiers."

In spite of the disparity in numbers the Christians rushed upon the enemy as a herd of deer hasten to quench their thirst in running water.[1] The leaders asserted that more than 100,000 of the enemy perished in battle or in flight. Unfortunately the city of Ascalon was not captured because of a quarrel between Godfrey and Raymond, each being determined to secure the city for his own possession.[2] The victory, however, was decisive. The leaders ascribed it to God's aid, and related how even the animals had assisted them. "On the day preceding the battle the army captured many thousands of camels, oxen and sheep. By command of the princes these were divided among the people. When we advanced to battle, wonderful to relate, the camels formed in many squadrons and the sheep and oxen did the same. Moreover, these animals accompanied us, halting when we halted, advancing when we advanced, and charging when we charged. The clouds protected us from the heat of the sun and cooled us."

Shortly after this battle Raymond, the two Roberts, their followers, and many others of the Crusaders left Jerusalem, most of them to return home. Godfrey and Tancred were left with only a very small force to defend the Christian possessions in Palestine. They were too few in number to make further conquests, and would have had difficulty even in defending Jerusalem against attack; but during the autumn of

[1] According to Lane-Poole, *History of Egypt*, VI, 164, the Franks surprised the enemy and attacked them in spite of a flag of truce.
[2] According to Lane-Poole, *ibid.*, Ascalon bribed the Franks to let it alone.

1099 the Muslims made no attempt, as they were thoroughly demoralized by their recent defeat.

In December came Dagobert, the papal legate, with many Tuscan and Italian followers. With him also came Bohemond from Antioch and Baldwin from Edessa, each accompanied by an armed band. For Bohemond had invited Baldwin to accompany him so that they might fulfill their vow and spend Christmas in the Holy City. They remained in Palestine only two weeks, but during their brief stay important events took place. Dagobert was chosen as patriarch in place of Arnulf, who had to yield, but as a compensation was made archdeacon of the church in Jerusalem. Godfrey and Bohemond became vassals of the patriarch *"propter amorem Dei,"* the one for Jerusalem, the other for Antioch. Bishops were ordained for the four cities of Tarsus, Mamistra, Artasia, and Edessa.

The hand of Bohemond can be seen in these transactions. When Dagobert came to Laodicea with one hundred twenty Pisan vessels, Bohemond induced him to take part in the siege of the city. Raymond of Toulouse and his followers arrived at Laodicea shortly afterwards, and persuaded Dagobert to withdraw from the siege, alleging that Bohemond was attacking a Christian city merely to bring it under his own power. Deprived of the aid of the Pisans, Bohemond was obliged to give up the siege and saw Raymond, his bitter enemy, welcomed into the city as its lord. Nevertheless he showed no animosity against Dagobert and even consented to a reconciliation with Raymond, which was arranged by the archbishop. Later, as stated above, he accompanied Dagobert to Jerusalem to fulfill his vow as a Crusader. It is possible that the vow weighed less heavily in the scale than did Bohemond's need for a valid title to the city of Antioch. He had secured it and was holding it in spite of the opposition of Raymond and many others, who insisted that in accordance with the oath made by the crusading leaders at Constantinople, Antioch ought to be given back to Emperor Alexius. Many felt that Bohemond was forsworn and had no right to the city. By becoming a vassal of the patriarch he secured a title to Antioch, and was in practically the same position to the patriarch that his father Robert Guiscard was in relation to the pope for his possessions in Southern Italy. Moreover, he obtained this without hampering in any degree his own power, as the patriarch of Jerusalem was too far away to interfere with the affairs of Antioch.

It was very different in the case of Godfrey. The patriarch was close at hand and was determined to rule; but Godfrey could make no effective opposition to Dagobert's claims, as the latter was supported by his Pisans and by Bohemond. Arnulf of Rohes was in a similar position and had to yield as gracefully as possible, but he was bitterly incensed and was only biding his time to become openly hostile to Dagobert. It is worthy of note that Baldwin did not become a vassal of the patriarch, and did not feel it necessary to get a more valid title to his county of Edessa. After spending only ten days in Jerusalem, Bohemond and

Baldwin left on January 1, 1100, to make their pilgrimage to the Jordan, and four days later started on the return journey to their homes in the North.

The new patriarch considered himself the head of both the church and the lay power. In a letter, written in April, 1100, to all Christians in Germany begging for assistance, he does not even mention Godfrey, but tells of his own difficulties in securing men to defend Jerusalem, Bethlehem, Joppa, Tiberias, Sebaste, Hebron, Ramlah, and the other fortresses which the Christians held. If we could trust the letter of Dagobert to Bohemond, which is given in William of Tyre's history, Godfrey was obliged at Easter, 1100, to take a new oath as vassal to the patriarch, and to promise to give up to him Jerusalem with its citadel, the Tower of David, and all Joppa, reserving only the administration and revenues of these cities until he had obtained other conquests. In addition, according to the same letter, he promised that if he died without an heir, the revenues from these cities should go to the patriarch. Even if the letter is genuine, the statements of the patriarch are open to some doubt, as he was stating his claims, and Godfrey was dead. Yet it is probable that some such action was taken at Easter, as the Pisans were still in Jerusalem at that time, and Godfrey had few followers.

During the first half of the year 1100 Godfrey did what he could with the feeble force at his command. With the aid of the Pisans he rebuilt Joppa, which they had found almost entirely destroyed. This was the seaport of Jerusalem, and it was necessary that the Christians should hold the city. But then, as now, the port was an open roadstead. Saewulf, who landed there in 1102, gives a vivid picture of the dangers both in landing and on the road from Joppa to Jerusalem, although he went over the road after it had been made safer by the exertions of Baldwin, to be mentioned later. After telling of his own fortunate landing, Saewulf describes a storm the following day:

"We had not looked at them long before the ships were driven from their anchors by the violence of the waves, which threw them now up aloft, and now down, until they were run aground or upon the rocks, and there they were beaten backwards and forwards until they were crushed to pieces. For the violence of the wind would not allow them to put out to sea, and the character of the coast would not allow them to put into shore with safety. Of the sailors and pilgrims who had lost all hope of escape, some remained on the ships, others laid hold of the masts or beams of wood; many remained in a state of stupor, and were drowned in that condition without any attempt to save themselves; some (although it may appear incredible) had in my sight their heads knocked off by the very timbers of the ships to which they had attached themselves for safety; others were carried out to sea on the beams, instead of being brought to land; even those who knew how to swim had not strength to struggle with the waves, and very few thus trusting to their own strength reached the shore alive. Thus, out of thirty very large ships, of which some were what are commonly called dromunds, some fulafres, and others cats, all laden with palmers and with merchandise, scarcely seven remained safe when we left the shore. Of persons of both sexes, there perished more than a thousand that day. Indeed, no eye ever beheld a greater misfortune in the space of a single day, from all which God snatched us by his grace; to whom be honour and glory forever. Amen.

"We went up from Joppa to the city of Jerusalem, a journey of two days, by a mountainous road, very rough, and dangerous on account of the Saracens, who lie in wait in caves of the mountains to surprise the Christians, watching both day and night to surprise those less capable of resisting by the smallness of their company, or the weary, who may chance to lag behind their companions. At one moment, you see them on every side; at another, they are altogether invisible, as may be witnessed by anybody travelling there. Numbers of human bodies lie scattered in the way, and by the wayside, torn to pieces by wild beasts. Some may, perhaps, wonder that the bodies of Christians are allowed to remain unburied, but it is not surprising when we consider that there is not much earth on the hard rock to dig a grave; and if earth were not wanting, who would be so simple as to leave his company and go alone to dig a grave for a companion? Indeed, if he did so he would rather be digging a grave for himself than for a dead man. For on that road, not only the poor and weak, but the rich and strong, are surrounded with perils; many are cut off by the Saracens, but more by heat and thirst;

PILGRIM ROAD FROM JAFFA TO JERUSALEM

many perish by the want of drink, but more by too much drinking. We, however, with all our company, reached the end of our journey."

Since the conditions at Joppa and on the road from there to Jerusalem were so bad, it was essential that the Crusaders should capture other seaports as speedily as possible. Tancred had taken possession of Tiberias in the autumn of 1099, and Godfrey had attempted the siege of Arsuf, but without result. In the following spring there were indecisive skirmishes between the Crusaders and the garrison at Arsuf. In spite of the enthusiastic account given in one of the chronicles, very little was accomplished during Godfrey's lifetime.

The desperate need of the Christians at Jerusalem is clearly evident from the terms made with the Venetian fleet, which came to Joppa in the summer of 1100. This was the first participation in the Crusade by Venice. Genoese ships had assisted at the sieges of Antioch and Jerusalem. The Pisans had come with Dagobert, and because of the grant made to him by Godfrey of a quarter of Joppa, a Pisan colony was later established there. The Venetians sold their aid only at a high price. They knew the weakness of Dagobert and Godfrey, making it impossible for the latter to capture any of the important seaports without the aid of a fleet. They bargained to aid the crusading hosts from June 24 to August 15, 1100, on condition that they should have a church and a market-place in every city, both on the seashore and in the interior, which the Christians held or might conquer. If any cities were captured jointly by the Crusaders and the Venetians, the latter should have one-third of the booty in each city. If Tripolis should be taken, the booty should be equally divided, and the Venetians should have the whole city, in return for a small annual payment, not to Godfrey, but to the Church of the Holy Sepulchre. In addition, the Venetians should be exempted from all taxes in all cities in the possession of Jerusalem, and no noble should have the right of flotsam and jetsam with regard to the goods in any Venetian vessel. After the agreement had been ratified the two parties may have planned to besiege Acre; if so, they soon changed their destination to Haifa, which was captured about August 20th, and given to Tancred.

The change in their plan is said to have been due to the death of Godfrey, on July 18th, after an illness of five weeks. There is no reason to suppose that he was not a victim of the pest, which was prevalent in Palestine that summer. But some of the contemporaries believed that he had been poisoned by the Mussulmans. It is significant, too, for the relations between him and the patriarch that one of the popular songs of the Crusade attributes the poisoning to Dagobert.

Godfrey had been defender of the Holy Sepulchre for less than a year, and had been able to accomplish very little. The people in the West, however, were deeply impressed with the success of the Crusade and the capture of Jerusalem. The popular imagination sought a hero and naturally found him in the brave

knight, the first ruler of Jerusalem. Soon legends
gathered about his name. First he was represented
as much more successful than he actually had been, as
having established a firm hold on the land, and as
receiving tribute from the Arabs, even in distant
cities, because of the terror inspired by his victories.
Many tales were told of his strength, bravery, and simplicity. For example, he cut off the head of a camel
with a single blow of his sword. His simplicity is
illustrated by a tale told of his siege of Arsuf, when
some deputies came from Samaria to offer him presents and found him seated on some straw on the
ground. He noticed their surprise and said the
ground might well serve as a seat during one's life
since it must be one's dwelling after death. Gradually
the tales grew until we have the Godfrey of the
legends, descended from the swan-knight, whose
glorious career as king of Jerusalem was revealed before his birth. At all events, Godfrey was a much
more heroic figure than Tancred, who was later glori-
fied as the hero of the First Crusade. While Godfrey
was not as able nor as powerful as either Bohemond
or Raymond, while he had few or none of the characteristics of a great leader, he was a brave and honest
man, not fanatical, but sincerely religious; not sel-
fishly seeking reward, but spending himself in the
common cause. The popular opinion was right; of
all the leaders of the First Crusade, Godfrey is the
most attractive and the most heroic.

After his death the patriarch hoped to have entire
control of Jerusalem, but Godfrey's followers refused

to deliver up the Tower of David and sent messengers to Edessa asking Baldwin to come and inherit his brother's property. This had been Godfrey's desire expressed on his deathbed in the presence of the patriarch and the leading nobles at Jerusalem. In order to counteract their plans, the patriarch wrote to his vassal Bohemond of Antioch. This letter is given in William of Tyre's history of the Crusade. Its genuineness has been much disputed and its terms often misstated. William of Tyre does not follow Albert of Aix, who is his most common source for the material for this period; he probably had access to a copy of the original letter. I think this is the case because of internal evidence. If William had manufactured this letter, as he frequently did other letters, he would have introduced his own ideas into it.

The letter of the patriarch recounts the various oaths taken by Godfrey and especially his promise to give up the city of Jerusalem if he died without an heir; the refusal of Godfrey's followers to do this and their obstinate retention of the Tower of David, "which causes greater evil to the Church than the tyranny of the Turks." He begs Bohemond to aid him and, in particular, to prevent Baldwin from coming to Jerusalem. There is no word about Bohemond's receiving the city of Jerusalem, as many secondary writers have asserted. I believe the letter to be genuine because it clearly shows the patriarch's purpose to be supreme in Jerusalem. It does not even hint that Bohemond should take the place of advocate of the Church of the Holy Sepulchre, left vacant by

Godfrey's death. These facts about the letter have been overlooked in the discussion of its genuineness. William of Tyre thought of Jerusalem as a kingdom, and he himself was the chancellor of the king; it seems improbable that he would have manufactured a letter that represented a point of view which he did not hold.

This letter was never received by Bohemond, because its bearer, the chaplain of the patriarch, was intercepted at Laodicea, and the letter was taken from him by some of the followers of Raymond, the bitter enemy of Bohemond. Later it was shown to Baldwin, whom it irritated strongly against the patriarch. Even if the letter had not been intercepted, the patriarch could have received no aid from Bohemond, as the latter had been captured by one of the Muslim emirs, and was held a prisoner.

In the meantime the messengers from Godfrey's followers had come to Edessa to seek Baldwin. The latter was a very different man from his brother. In his youth he had been trained as a clerk, and after somewhat extensive studies had received prebends in the churches of Rheims, Cambrai, and Limoges; but for unknown reasons he gave up his benefices, laid aside the clerical garb, and became a knight. As has been said, Baldwin had been invited by the Armenian ruler of Edessa to come to his aid and had been adopted by the aged prince and his wife as their son. We have little knowledge of what happened at Edessa after the adoption. Fulcher of Chartres, the chaplain of Baldwin, who has left such an excellent account of the First Crusade and the early years of the kingdom, is discreetly silent, and we may conclude that he had reason to be, in order not to tarnish the glory of his lord. At all events, after a short time the people of Edessa rebelled against the aged ruler and murdered him. Baldwin was accepted as their prince and consolidated his position by marrying an Armenian princess. He took no part in the capture of Antioch or Jerusalem, but remained at Edessa. In his appearance he was well fitted to be a ruler. He was much larger than Godfrey, and, like Saul, he towered a head above ordinary men. He had reddish brown hair and a beard of the same color, but a rather white complexion. His nose was aquiline, his upper lip prominent, and his lower teeth somewhat drawn back, but not sufficiently to make him look peculiar. He was neither too stout nor too thin. His ordinary dress made him appear more like a bishop than a layman, and this appearance was accentuated by his dignified bearing and serious countenance. He was much admired for his skill at arms and in managing a horse. He was active and brave, and possessed all the qualities hereditary in his family. This is the account given of him by William of Tyre, who notes only two faults: first, that he was too fond of women, although no scandals resulted, as his amours were known only to his servants; and, second, that he had too much confidence in Arnulf, of whom more later.

When the messengers arrived at Edessa about September 12th, Baldwin had just returned from an expedition undertaken to free Bohemond from captivity. When he heard the message, as Fulcher of Chartres relates, he grieved somewhat at the death of his brother, but rejoiced much more over the inheritance. He at once made preparations to go to Jerusalem, and, gathering an army of 200 knights and 700 foot-soldiers, set out on October 2nd. On his way he stopped at Antioch, which was without a lord, and whose inhabitants begged him to remain and accept the lordship. It is significant of his character and ambitions that he did not do so. Probably he was influenced somewhat by Bohemond's claims to the city and by the fact that the latter had many partisans, but if Baldwin had preferred Antioch, these reasons would not have deterred him. In spite of the superior wealth of Antioch, Baldwin seems to have realized the possibilities and prestige as ruler of Jerusalem. At Laodicea he met a Genoese fleet accompanied by a new papal legate. The latter urged him to take the crown at Jerusalem. Baldwin said he would, provided that the Genoese fleet would aid him to capture two cities, and this the Genoese promised. Possibly Baldwin thought of these two cities as an offset to Jerusalem and Joppa, which Godfrey had agreed to give to the patriarch if he secured other possessions. If so, Baldwin's ideas changed later. At Dog River, north of Beirut, he had hard fighting to get through the pass, and the army was in grave danger. Fulcher of Chartres in telling about the battle says: "I would have preferred to be at Chartres or Orleans rather than there; and others felt the same." By November 6th he reached Joppa, and about three days later Jerusalem. There he received a royal reception, in spite of the intrigues of Tancred, who had done all that he could to secure the city for the patriarch, to turn the inhabitants against Baldwin, and to prevent the latter's entry into the city. But Arnulf of Rohes had a strong party and had thrown in his lot with the followers of Godfrey. As Baldwin approached the city, he was met by a great procession of the citizens, Latin, Syrian, and Greek, who led him to the Holy Sepulchre, where he knelt in prayer, and then gave magnificent presents. The patriarch took no part in this demonstration, but remained aloof on Mount Zion.

A few days later Baldwin received the oaths of vassalage and fidelity from his new subjects. In order to increase his prestige, he then made an expedition to the south and southwest, and was successful in skirmishes with the enemy, especially near Ascalon. He made the roads safer for the pilgrims by massacring many troglodytes, whom he smoked out of the caves in which they took refuge. On December 21st he returned to Jerusalem, and on Christmas Day was crowned king at Bethlehem by Dagobert, with whom a reconciliation had been arranged. In his coronation oath he promised to show due reverence to the patriarch, and to protect the Church in the possession of its rights. We do not know the details of the reconciliation, but it is significant that the coronation was at Bethlehem and not at Jerusalem, and also that Baldwin did not take the title of king of Jerusalem.

For several years he styled himself simply king, or else king of Asia, or king of Asia and Babylon.

Baldwin's position at first was very difficult. Tancred with his forces had gone to Antioch to take charge of the city during Bohemond's captivity. The troops that remained at Baldwin's disposal were very few in number. Fulcher of Chartres tells us that to defend Jerusalem, Joppa, Ramlah, and Haifa there were only 300 knights and the same number of foot-soldiers, and he expresses his wonder that so many hundreds of thousands of enemies did not unite, and "were afraid to attack our little kingdom and our few people." In addition to the lack of union among his opponents, Baldwin was strengthened by the accession of armed bands of pilgrims who came each year to visit the Holy Sepulchre and to bathe in the Jordan, and to spend a few weeks or months fighting the infidel; e.g., in February, 1101, William, count of Nevers, set out for Jerusalem with 1500 knights and foot-soldiers. In March of the same year William, count of Poitou, with a large following from Aquitaine and Gascony, also set out for the Holy City. In the same month the Genoese fleet arrived at Haifa from Laodicea.

With the fleet came the new papal legate, by whom Patriarch Dagobert is said to have been temporarily suspended from his office on the charges that he had attempted to have Bohemond assassinate Baldwin on the latter's march to Jerusalem, and that he had been too prodigal in giving away fragments of the True Cross. This suspension, if it happened, was undoubt-

edly the work of Arnulf and his party, and freed
Baldwin from the interference of the patriarch for
a time. Another event took place this same spring
which was destined to have fortunate results in lessening the power of the patriarch. On Saturday in
Holy Week all the inhabitants of Jerusalem were
gathered in the Church of the Holy Sepulchre to
witness the miracle of the Holy Fire, but the miracle
did not take place. When night came, the Latins
withdrew in dismay. The following morning the
king, the legate, and the people made a solemn procession. While they were absent and while only the
Greek and Syrian clergy were in the Holy Sepulchre,
the fire appeared. We get a hint from one of the native chroniclers, who tells us that God was angry
because the Greek priests had been deprived of their
rights in the Holy Sepulchre, and women had been
introduced into the monasteries. As a result of negotiations with the king, the Greeks were restored to
their positions in the church, women were expelled
from the monasteries, and God, appeased, sent down
the Holy Fire. The restoration of the Greeks was
symptomatic of Baldwin's policy. He did all that he
could to attach the natives to his interests. He offered
freedom of trade and residence in Jerusalem to people
of all creeds in order to build up the prosperity of the
city. He showed himself merciful on occasion to prisoners and made agreements with some of the enemy
cities. This policy was to be followed not only by
Baldwin but also by his successors. It is very interesting to get the testimony of Muslims as to its suc-

cess. The relations between the Christians and the infidels were frequently good, as is attested later by Usamah, Ibn-Jubayr, and many others.

This policy did not preclude warlike undertakings whenever Baldwin had sufficient forces. He utilized the presence of the Genoese fleet, which he had met at Joppa, to attack and capture Arsuf, April 29, and Caesarea, May 17, 1101. His position was so much stronger than had been that of Godfrey the preceding year that he was able to make much more satisfactory terms with the Genoese. He agreed to give them a section in each city which might be conquered with their aid, and one-third of the booty. The capture of Caesarea was especially important. This had been a much more flourishing city under the Muslim rule than it was later. The booty was enormous. The Genoese received one-third of it, and this was so great that each one of the 8000 sailors in the fleet had as his share forty-eight solidi of Poitou and two pounds of pepper. The king's share, twice as great as that of the Genoese, gave him large funds to pay followers. At Caesarea also, as part of the booty, was secured a costly green hexagonal vase, which was later believed to be the Holy Grail. One incident of the victory is eloquent of the age. This is the burning of great heaps of the bodies of the slain in order to obtain the gold which the victims were believed to have concealed by swallowing.

The need for money was an ever-present anxiety with Baldwin, and soon brought on a new conflict with the patriarch, from whom he demanded a contribution to help pay for his soldiers. The patriarch agreed at first, but did not keep his promise. There was no possibility of peace between the two, and finally in 1102 Dagobert was deposed by a church council under the presidency of a new papal legate, and had to leave the city. Under Arnulf's influence a simple, pious parish priest named Evremar was chosen patriarch. From this time on Baldwin had no opposition to fear from the patriarch to his claim to be ruler of Jerusalem. In 1104 we find him for the first time using the style, King of Jerusalem. The feudal kingdom was established.

Baldwin's chaplain, Fulcher of Chartres, defends his master for accepting the crown of gold which Godfrey had not worn, and which so many of the clergy felt to be unfitting in Jerusalem, where Christ had worn a crown of thorns. Fulcher argues that no one is anointed king except by the will of God. When a king accepts the office and the crown of gold he binds himself to administer justice. If he does not rule righteously he is no king. This thesis was in accordance with the political theory of the twelfth century. It was given the fullest expression by John of Salisbury, the secretary of Thomas Becket. In his *Policraticus,* or *Statesman's Book,* he develops this idea at length and draws a contrast between a king who works for the good of his subjects and a tyrant who tramples justice underfoot. He sums up his argument, "The prince is in a way the image of the Divinity; the tyrant is the image of violence which is in revolt against God, and of perversity, the daughter of hell As the image of Divinity the prince ought to be loved, venerated, and obeyed; as the image of diabolical perversity the tyrant ought in most cases to be put to death.' Fulcher felt that Baldwin was the just king, "the image of Divinity," and not the tyrant and therefore might wear a crown of gold in Jerusalem.

Before I conclude this chapter, there is one other subject that should be discussed. This is the origin of the Assizes of Jerusalem. In the first chapter of the first book of the Assizes of the High Court it is stated that these were drawn up by commissioners appointed by Godfrey. They were instructed to inquire and ascertain of the Crusaders from the different countries the usages in their lands. When the commissioners reported in writing, Godfrey and his council chose what was suitable, and a code was drawn up which became the Assizes and Usages for the Kingdom of Jerusalem. This code, sealed with the seals of Godfrey, the patriarch, and the viscount of Jerusalem, was placed in the Church of the Holy Sepulchre, and hence it was sometimes called "the letters of the Sepulchre." Whenever a doubtful point was raised in a court in Palestine, this record was consulted with due solemnity in the presence of nine persons representing the various interests: royal, ecclesiastical, feudal, and bourgeois. It was lost when Saladin captured Jerusalem in 1187.

If this story were true, we should have to draw a very different picture of the establishment of the Latin kingdom of Jerusalem. As a matter of fact there is no truth whatever in the tale. No such collection was drawn up under Godfrey's direction, there was no viscount of Jerusalem during his lifetime, and there is no record of the consultation of any such code. Instead, William of Tyre tells us twice that when any question of usage arose under Baldwin III or Amalric I—both his contemporaries—the king was appealed to because of his profound knowledge of the customary law. No such code was in existence to be lost in 1187. The truth is that the story was made up by Jean d'Ibelin, more than a century after the death of Godfrey, in order to give greater prestige to the code of assizes which he had himself collected from the memory of older men. This fact is now acknowledged by students of the Crusades, although some of them very illogically, and without any basis of source-material, try to rescue a part of the tale by transferring it into something else. Others, curiously enough, do not hesitate to use these assizes as historical sources for a period anterior to their redaction.

CHAPTER IV

THE KINGDOM AT ITS ZENITH

AFTER describing an eclipse of the sun in 1124, Fulcher of Chartres writes, "Why should it be wondered at that God shows signs in the heavens when he has wrought a great miracle on earth in turning the Occidentals into Orientals? ... Consider, I pray, and reflect how in our time God has transferred the West into the East. For we who were Occidentals now have been made Orientals. He who was a Roman or a Frank is now a Galilaean, or an inhabitant of Palestine. One who was a citizen of Rheims or of Chartres now has been made a citizen of Tyre or of Antioch. We have already forgotten the places of our birth; already they have become unknown to many of us, or, at least, are unmentioned. Some already possess here homes and servants which they have received through inheritance. Some have taken wives not merely of their own people, but Syrians, or Armenians, or even Saracens who have received the grace of baptism. Some have with them father-in-law, or daughter-in-law, or son-in-law, or step-son, or step-father. There are here, too, grandchildren and great-grandchildren. One cultivates vines, another the fields. The one and the other use mutually the speech and the idioms of the different languages. Different languages, now made common, become known to both races, and faith unites those whose forefathers were strangers. As it is written, 'The lion and the ox shall eat straw together.' Those who were strangers are now natives; and he who was a sojourner now has become a resident. Our parents and relatives from day to day come to join us, abandoning, even though reluctantly, all that they possess. For those who were poor there, here God makes rich. Those who had few coins, here possess countless besants; and those who had not had a villa, here, by the gift of God, already possess a city. Therefore, why should one who has found the East so favorable return to the West? God does not wish those to suffer want who, carrying their crosses, have vowed to follow Him, nay even unto the end. You see, therefore, that this is a great miracle, and one which must greatly astonish the whole world. Who has ever heard anything like it? Therefore, God wishes to enrich us all and to draw us to Himself as His most dear friends." This description may be taken as a summary of the work of the first two kings—conquest and assimilation.

After the deposition of Dagobert, Baldwin I had little trouble with the church, to which he made large grants of land and serfs. In time of need he could expect the aid of the patriarch. When, in August, 1105, the ruler of Egypt sent a great host of Arabians, Ethiopians, and Turks against Baldwin, the king sent to the patriarch for aid. The latter hastily raised a force of 150 horse and foot in Jerusalem and led them in person to Ramlah. Only those who were unfit for fighting remained in the Holy City, and they devoted themselves to prayers, alms-giving, and fasting. The mothers even refused to nurse their babies until the ninth hour of the day (about the middle of the afternoon). In 1112 Arnulf, who had been very influential under the preceding patriarchs, himself received the patriarchate and continued to work in harmony with the king.

Baldwin's position in the early years of his reign was a desperate one. As Fulcher had said, there were very few soldiers, and they were constantly exposed to attack. On the south the Egyptians held Ascalon, and it was easy for them to harry the Christians. Ramlah, with a garrison of only fifteen knights, was the Christian outpost to ward off this danger, and repeatedly the fields nearby were drenched with blood. In 1102 Ramlah was captured by the Egyptian ruler and held for a time. On the east the land lay open to invasion at any time. From the Christians in the north no help could be expected, as they were occupied in defending their own territories and extending their conquests. On the coast most of the important cities were still in the hands of the Muslims. The inhabitants of Jerusalem and the surrounding country were few. The pilgrims who came from the West were so oppressed by the desolation of the land and the dangers they encountered that they hastened to complete their pilgrimages and to return home.

Baldwin was constantly active in military expeditions to acquire booty, to make conquests, or to ward off threatened danger. At times he made a raid and captured many prisoners to be sold as slaves; in one expedition 4000 camels and great wealth were secured. At times he began a siege of one of the seaports but raised the siege on the payment of a large sum, as from Tyre in 1108. He was always in need of men and of money to pay for their services. Fortunately pilgrims flocked to the Holy Land each year, and some of them could be induced to fight for the cause of the Lord. Most important were the fleets which came almost yearly. In 1102 there were 200 ships from England which arrived just in time to save Baldwin from the results of one of his daring attacks upon forces far outnumbering his own. The help of the fleets from the Italian cities was most important, and almost all of the captures of seaports were made with their aid. The Genoese were the most active and assisted at the capture of Caesarea, Tortosa, Acre, and Tripolis. Such fleets came usually in the summer, but during the rainy season there was little danger from enemies and little opportunity to make expeditions. One Muslim leader who attempted an attack was delayed two months by rain and snow.

The Fatimite caliph of Egypt was very energetic in his attempt to crush the Christians, and Baldwin met with frequent defeats by his forces, especially in 1102 and 1103. Fortunately for the Franks, the other Muslims were usually at enmity with the Egyptians and also were at strife with one another. They frequently entered into alliances with the Crusaders, and Muslim and Christian fought against Christian or Muslim opponents; very often men of the two faiths were engaged on both sides. Some of the Muslim rulers were very glad to have the Crusaders in the land, for without their presence they would have found it difficult, if not impossible, to keep their own possessions.

Fighting with a single enemy at a time, one seaport after another was captured, Acre and Jubayl in 1104, Tripolis in 1109, Beirut and Sidon in 1110, the latter with the help of Sigurd of Norway and the Venetians. In these captures frequently great cruelty and brutality was shown; on more than one occasion the inhabitants were slaughtered after they had received safe-conduct to leave the city, and their bodies were burned or cut open to secure the gold which they were supposed to have swallowed.

Similar brutality was exercised by the Turks upon their captives. In 1108 Tughtakin captured Guy of Bazochez, Baldwin's nephew, and offered to ransom him if the king would give up Acre, Haifa, and Tiberias. The king declared that he would never give up any captured city but offered 30,000 pieces of gold and 500 captives in exchange for Guy. Tughtakin refused, and, as Guy had refused to become a Muslim, had his head cut off and the skull made into a drinking cup.

In 1113 Baldwin was relieved from his constant anxiety about money because he was able to marry advantageously. As we have already heard he had lost his first wife on the march to Antioch and had married Arda, an Armenian princess, at Edessa. She was repudiated on the ground of misconduct, and Baldwin was free to sue for the hand of Adelaide, widow of Duke Roger of Sicily. She came with a fleet of nine vessels, 1000 warriors, and many Muslim archers, a huge treasure of money, weapons, and supplies. It was agreed that if Baldwin died without an heir, her son Roger should succeed to the kingdom of Jerusalem. In 1117 Baldwin, believing himself on the point of death, repented of the wrong he had done Arda and sent Adelaide home, divorced on the grounds of consanguinity, but in the meantime her money had been very useful. In 1115 the castle of Montreal had been built beyond the Jordan to command the caravan road, and in 1117 Scandalion was built between Tyre and Acre to protect the road along the coast. In 1116 Baldwin had led a force as far as Elim on the Red Sea, and this port remained in the possession of the Christians until 1170.

In the north the fortunes of the Christians had varied. After the captivity of Bohemond,[1] Tancred had been made regent of Antioch. This principality included northern Syria and Cilicia with the important cities of Tarsus, Mamistra, and Adana. On the northeast it was protected by Edessa, although the two Christian states were often at enmity. On all other fronts it was exposed to attacks, especially by Emperor Alexius, who had the ports of Laodicea, Valania, and Maraclea to the south and was eager

[1] See Chapter III.

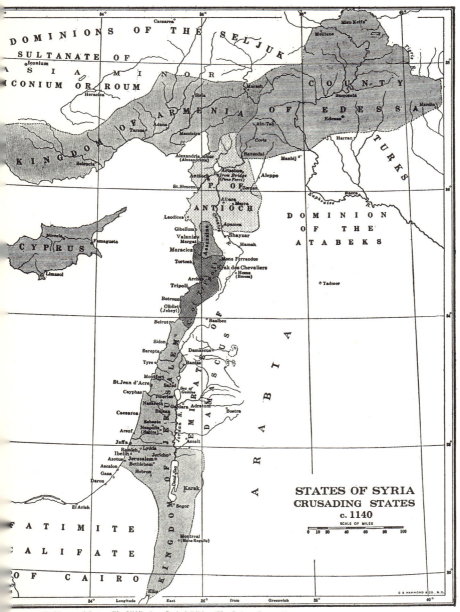

STATES OF SYRIA
CRUSADING STATES
c. 1140

SCALE OF MILES

0   10   20   40   60   80   100

to recover Cilicia. Fortunately for the Franks the country to the east was held by the weak ruler of Aleppo and independent or semi-independent chiefs such as the lord of Shayzar, who were seldom ready to unite their forces against the Crusaders. Tancred was very active, especially against the Greeks, from whom he captured Laodicea. He does not seem to have been anxious to have Bohemond freed from captivity and contributed not a penny to his ransom which was raised, in 1103, mainly by the patriarch of Antioch, by Baldwin of Edessa, Tancred's enemy, and by an Armenian lord. After his release Bohemond attacked the possessions of Aleppo. In one campaign in which he was aiding Baldwin of Edessa the latter was captured and Tancred was made regent of Edessa. A little later Bohemond and Tancred had an opportunity to exchange one of their prisoners, a Turkish matron, for Baldwin but refused and accepted a ransom of 15,000 gold pieces for the matron in spite of the effort of King Baldwin to get them to exchange her for the count of Edessa.

In the ensuing months the fortunes of the Christians in the north became desperate. They were attacked at the same time by Turks and Greeks. Bohemond determined to go to Europe to raise a force against Alexius and left Tancred in command of both Antioch and Edessa. The following years were, in spite of many set-backs, fortunate for Tancred. He used skillfully the dissensions of the Turks and made some conquests. To oppose him the Turks released Baldwin, who, in spite of Tancred's opposition, recovered Edessa. Each of them made alliances with the Turks against the other. The Greek emperor attempted to form an alliance with the caliph at Bagdad against Tancred. Yet the latter held his possessions in the principality and conquered more territory. In 1107 he was able to recover Cilicia, which the emperor had conquered, because the latter was busy with Bohemond who had brought a huge force from the West to attack the Greek empire. When Tancred died in 1112 his nephew, Roger, succeeded to the power in Antioch. He was a bold warrior and in alliance with some Turkish rulers won a great victory in 1115. For a time this made the Franks predominant. "They spread their arms to the east of Aleppo," says an Arabic historian, "they laid waste the province, and attacked Aleppo itself. That city would have been deserted had its inhabitants known where to find safety."

In the meantime at Edessa the inhabitants had suffered greatly. In 1105 they revolted against the cruel rule of Tancred. After Baldwin's release, in spite of his greed and in spite of attacks and siege by the Turks, things went better, and Baldwin seems to have been feared and respected, if not loved.

During this period also the county of Tripolis was gradually being formed. Raymond of Toulouse had taken an oath to Tancred not to make any conquests to the south of Antioch, but he sought nevertheless to capture Tripolis and built the castle of Mont-Pèlerin. He died in 1105 while engaged in the siege of Tripolis. His son, Bertram, came to Syria to claim his father's possessions but was opposed by his cousin William Jordan who had succeeded Raymond. William appealed to Tancred for aid and Bertram to King Baldwin. The latter arranged a compromise and division of territory, and the united forces captured Tripolis in 1109. William's opportune and mysterious death left Bertram count of Tripolis. Its capital, the city of Tripolis, was a square of a thousand cubits, and on three sides it was washed by the sea; on the fourth side there was a wall with a moat. A Persian who visited the city about fifty years before the First Crusade writes, "The city measures 1,000 cubits long, by the like across. Its hostelries are four and five stories high, and there are even some that are six. The private houses and bazaars are well built, and so clean that one might take each to be a palace for its splendour. Every kind of meat, and fruit, and eatable that ever I saw in all the land of Persia is to be had here, and a hundred degrees better in quality.... They say there are twenty thousand men in this city, and the place possesses many territories and villages. They make here very good paper, like that of Samarkand, only of better quality." Another Persian traveller who wrote after it had been in the possession of the Christians for about fifty years says Tripolis "is a great city, defended by a stone wall, and impregnable. It has villages, and territories, and fine domains; and many trees such as olives, vines, sugar-cane, and fruit-trees of all kinds, and of all manner of crops a variety beyond count. Coming and going there is perpetual. The sea embraces the town on three sides, and it is one of the great fortresses of Syria. All sorts of wares are brought thither, and of stuffs and merchandise great quantities." Both are describing the old city of Al-Mina or Tripoli Marine. The new town had grown up near the castle of Raymond. In the last days of the Christian occupation it was said to contain 4000 looms for weaving silk.[2]

King Baldwin won prestige by his success in reconciling all the adversaries at Tripolis, and he commanded the respect of his enemies by his bravery and energy. His reputation is well illustrated by the attitude of the Fatimite caliph; on the news of Baldwin's illness in 1117 he despatched a fleet against the Crusaders' seaports, but on hearing of the king's recovery he recalled the fleet before it had made an attack. Unfortunately the same year was marked by great trials for the kingdom: in May a plague of locusts, in June an eclipse of the moon and also an earthquake, in December an eclipse of the sun. The Christians awaited anxiously the meaning of these portents in the heavens. They learned the meaning when not only Baldwin died, April 2, 1118, but also the same year the caliph, the sultan, Emperor Alexius, and Pope Paschal II. Fortunately Baldwin by his constant activity had laid the foundation of the kingdom securely and was succeeded by an able king, Baldwin II.

Baldwin du Bourg had participated in the capture

---

[2] About two and a half miles from Tripolis is a famous convent built by a pool which contains sacred fish. According to a local legend these fish are sacred because they fought against the Crusaders.

of Antioch and Jerusalem and, remaining in the East, had entered the service of Bohemond. He was a nephew of Baldwin I and, when the latter became king, succeeded him as count of Edessa. He had planned to spend Easter day, 1118, in Jerusalem and entered the city just in time to meet the funeral procession of Baldwin I. As he was on the spot, he was chosen king instead of Eustace, brother of Baldwin I, who was in Europe, and was crowned on Easter day.

The new king was a man of lofty stature, comely features, and ruddy complexion. He was already advanced in years but bore them lightly and was a bold, hardy warrior. Unlike his predecessor he was a wary, prudent general. He was very devout; his hands and knees were said to have been calloused from frequent prayers, and he often carried the Holy Cross on his military expeditions. His long rule at Edessa had made him well acquainted with the character of the natives and their methods of warfare. He had, on the whole, been well liked by his subjects and respected by his enemies, both Muslim and Christian. It was the support of one of the latter who, putting aside his feeling of personal enmity, had advised the choice of Baldwin that was decisive in securing for him the succession to the throne.

His task was a difficult one. The Muslims were more united than before and Il Ghazi, ruler of Aleppo, had concluded an alliance with the sultan of Egypt. This in turn caused a greater unity among the Christians. To meet the threatened attack of Il

Ghazi, Roger of Antioch called for aid from Joscelin of Edessa, the count of Tripolis, and King Baldwin, but without waiting for the king went out to meet the enemy. His forces were defeated and he was killed. Few of the Christians escaped slaughter or capture, and all of the captives were killed except a few who were believed capable of paying a large ransom. The city of Antioch was left almost without defenders, but the patriarch took energetic action to man the walls and sent a pressing call for aid to Baldwin. He hastened to Antioch where, in an assemblage of the clergy and people, it was decided that he should take the principality under his protection until Bohemond II should be of age and that Bohemond then should marry one of the king's daughters. The defences of the city were strengthened, the widows of the knights who had fallen with Roger were given in marriage to others, and other necessary arrangements were made.

The following year, 1120, was marked by the holding of the Council of Nabulus (Neapolis). For four years the land had suffered severely from swallows, locusts, and mice, from famine and epidemics, from earthquakes and signs in the heavens. To these were added the new dangers from the Muslims, so that the patriarch decided to attempt to avert God's wrath by a reformation of morals. The Council met in January and was attended by most of the clergy and many nobles. The king granted to the church a tithe from all of the income of the kingdom and from any lands that might be added to it. He and his nobles restored all the tithes which they had withheld and received absolution. Heavy penalties were enacted for adulteɪy, bigamy, and theft as well as for members of the clergy who were untrue to their vows. In order to secure more ample supplies for Jerusalem the king removed all dues on wares entering or leaving the city and allowed the natives, both Christian and Muslim, to bring provisions for sale free from tax. The Franks considered some success in that year a sign that God's wrath had been appeased by the reformation of morals; possibly also they felt the same when they learned of the murder of the grand vizier of Egypt the following year, as this resulted in a lessening of danger from attack. In 1122 Il Ghazi also died, but the capture of Joscelin that year and of Baldwin II in the following year weakened the Franks, who on the whole had had the upper hand in the fighting up to that time.

Both Baldwin and Joscelin were imprisoned at Kharput. Thither, according to the account by Fulcher, came about fifty Armenians pretending that they were merchants and gained admission to the city. Under the pretext of complaining of unjust treatmènt they sought the commandant, whom they found playing chess. Drawing their knives they killed him. Hastily seizing lances which they found there, they killed the Turkish guard and freed Joscelin and Baldwin and ran up a Christian banner on the tower. The city was soon besieged by the Turks, but Joscelin succeeded in escaping and, travelling by night, reached the Euphrates almost barefooted. On the farther bank he concealed himself while one of his attendants sought food. The latter found an Armenian peasant who had some figs and grapes and led him to Joscelin. The peasant recognized him and offered his services without pay, as Joscelin had formerly befriended him. Joscelin, dressed in the clothes of the peasant's wife and mounted upon an ass, carrying the peasant's baby girl in his arms, set out for Turbessel (Tell Bashir). Unfortunately the baby wished to nurse and cried lustily. Joscelin did not want to carry her, but he was persuaded by the peasant that it was necessary for his safety. He succeeded in his escape and hastened to Antioch and Jerusalem to secure aid for the king. He was too late, for in the meantime Kharput had been recaptured by the Turks and Baldwin had been taken to Harran for more safe keeping.

As soon as the Egyptians heard of Baldwin's capture they began preparations to attack Joppa. The city was defended with desperate bravery by both men and women and finally rescued by a force from Jerusalem. An urgent request for aid had been sent to a Venetian fleet which was on its way in answer to an appeal which Baldwin had sent after the death of Roger. The fleet was a strong one and when it came to Joppa offered to aid in the capture of some seaport. After hesitation between Ascalon and Tyre, the lot, drawn by an innocent orphan boy, fell for Tyre. The Venetians were guaranteed one-third of the city, if captured, and of the surrounding territory, a quarter in Jerusalem equal in size to that held by the king, and freedom of trade without any tolls in all the kingdom, as well as special juridical privileges in Tyre. The siege, both by land and water, began on February 15, 1124. The city was renowned for its wealth, for its houses of five and even six stories, for its strong defenses—on the land side a single gate, on the sea a single entrance protected by two towers between which a chain could be stretched to prevent ingress. In spite of a brave defense and aid attempted by both Tughtakin and the caliph of Egypt, the city had to capitulate on July 7th, as the inhabitants were almost starved.

Great was the joy throughout the kingdom at this victory, and the joy was enhanced when news came that Baldwin had been released. It was at this time that Fulcher wrote the words quoted at the beginning of this chapter. The king did not keep his promise to pay the ransom, alleging that the patriarch had forbidden it. The remaining years of Baldwin's reign witnessed desultory fighting and alliances with the infidel but were marked especially by the death of the two most important Muslim leaders and by the coming of Bohemond II to take charge of Antioch and of Fulk of Anjou to be Baldwin's successor; each of them married a daughter of the king. Baldwin died in 1131 after having put on a monk's garb. Under him the kingdom reached its greatest extent and power. From the pen of a Muslim we have the best picture of his success. Ibn-al-Athir writes that the Franks were everywhere feared, only Aleppo, Hims, Hamah, and Damascus remained in the hands of the true believers; Aleppo had to pay one-half of its income; Damascus had to submit to visits from Christian agents who released all Christian slaves who desired their liberty; the other cities were in still worse state.

One of the legists in the kingdom of Jerusalem explained the position of the king by stating that the kingdom was not, like some other states, conquered by one prince who might have considered himself the complete lord of its destiny, but that it was won by an army of pilgrims gathered together from all Christian lands under the leadership of God, and the first king was elected. As we have seen, there was at first a question whether any one ought to be chosen king, and there was a struggle with the patriarch who desired to be head of the state, but Baldwin made himself supreme. On the other hand, the church was endowed with numerous possessions and was required to furnish very few soldiers in comparison with its feudal holdings. It did much for charity, but little for the defense of the kingdom, and still less to maintain the morale. The decline of the kingdom has frequently been attributed to the vices of the Franks, in which the clergy shared.

The king's household was modelled after those in the West, with seneschal, constable, marshal, chamberlain, and chancellor. His immediate domain included Jerusalem with the surrounding territory and the cities of Acre and Tyre. All the other conquests had been given out as fiefs, some before the accession of Baldwin I. There were eventually four great baronies and twelve lesser fiefs held from the king, but the vassals were turbulent and sometimes flouted the king's authority.

In order to hold the country and to extend his dominions, the king's greatest need was more recruits from the West. The number of soldiers in the service of the kingdom was never large—never more than a few hundred knights and a few thousand foot-soldiers —and these numbers were constantly fluctuating as the pilgrims returned home after a single campaign in the East. Many letters were written, and much advertising was done in order to secure more recruits. The popes were insistent that all who had taken the cross and were capable of fighting should fulfill their vow. Stephen of Blois, who had fled from Antioch, was compelled by the force of public opinion to go on the Crusade of 1101 and met his death. Ordericus Vitalis writes, "Being frequently reproved by a variety of persons for this conduct, Stephen was compelled both by fear and shame to undertake a fresh Crusade. Among others, his wife, Adele, often urged him to it, reminding him of it even amidst the endearments of conjugal caresses. 'Far be it from me, my lord,' she said, 'to submit any longer to the jibes you receive from all quarters. Pluck up the courage for which you were renowned in your youth, and take arms in a noble cause for the salvation of thousands, so that Christians may have good reason to exult in all parts of the world, to the terror of the pagans and the public humiliation of their detestable religion.'

"This was the sort of language that clever and spirited woman often addressed to her husband. He certainly had already sufficiently experienced the perils and difficulties of the enterprise to make him shrink from undergoing such toils again. At length, however, he took courage, and, putting himself on the march at the head of many thousand French, persevered against most formidable obstacles, until he reached the tomb of our Lord."

In order to secure the services of fighting men the king had to develop a new kind of fief, not based on land, but on payments in money or kind. Thus we have instances, later, where a knight is hired to serve with four horses and receives 200 bezants, 50 measures of wheat, 20 measures of barley, 10 measures of beans, 50 measures of oil annually. By such means the king built up a small standing army, and his effective forces were increased because, unlike the West where the feudal services were exacted for only forty days each year, in the Holy Land the requirement was one year each year. But even when all the vassals fulfilled their services the total number on which the king could nominally count was only about 700 knights and 5000 foot-soldiers. The Italians, who had received so many privileges, were not obliged to serve in the king's army but did have to assist in the defense of the seaports in which they had quarters.

A great aid to the king came from the foundation of the Templars. About 1119 a pilgrim, Hugh de Payen, associated with himself eight other knights to form "the poor fellow soldiers of Christ" to protect pilgrims on their journey in the Holy Land. Baldwin II gave them a residence near the Temple of Solomon, and they soon came to be known as Templars or Knights of the Temple. They took the monastic vows, but not necessarily for life, and also a vow to fight for the protection of pilgrims and of the Holy Land. In 1127 Hugh went to France to obtain aid. At the Council of Troyes in the following year, the new order was sanctioned and received the mighty support of Bernard of Clairvaux, who wrote enthusiastically, "They live together without separate property, in one house, under one rule, careful to preserve the unity of the spirit in the bond of peace. Never is an idle word, or useless deed, or immoderate laughter, or a murmur, if it be but whispered, allowed to go unpunished. Draughts and dice they detest. Hunting they hold in abomination; and take no pleasure in the frivolous pastime of hawking. Soothsayers, jesters, and story-tellers, ribald songs and stage plays they eschew as insane follies. They cut close the hair, knowing, as the Apostle says, that 'it is a shame for a man to have long hair.' They never dress gaily, and wash but seldom. Shaggy by reason of their uncombed hair, they are also begrimed with dust, and swarthy from the weight of their armour and the heat of the sun. They strive earnestly to possess strong and swift horses, but not garnished with ornaments or decked with trappings, thinking of battle and victory, not of pomp and show. Such hath God chosen for His own, who vigilantly and faithfully guard the Holy Sepulchre, all armed with the sword, and most learned in the art of war." In the thirteenth century, Jacques de Vitry, who had been long enough resident in Palestine to speak from personal knowledge, says: "When the Templars were called to arms, they did not ask how many of the enemy there were, but where they were. They were lions in war, and gentle as lambs at home; in the field they were fierce soldiers, in church they were like hermits or monks; they were harsh and savage to the enemies of Christ, but kindly and gracious to Christians. They had a black and white banner, which they called *Bauceant,* borne before them, signifying that they are fair and kindly to their friends, but black and terrible to their enemies."

Gifts poured in for the Order. The motley garb of charity was replaced by a white mantle for the knights, and a few years later the pope authorized all Templars to bear the red cross. They soon became a very prominent factor in the defense of the land. They acquired enormous wealth, mainly from their possessions in the west of Europe and through commerce, but were wholly independent of the authority of king or patriarch, owing obedience only to the pope.

The Knights of the Hospital sprang from an older foundation, at first devoted to caring for poor pilgrims. Following the example of the Templars, they too became a military order, acquired wealth in many lands, and held only from the pope. These two orders were in their early years a great source of strength; later they frequently quarreled with each other, and sometimes were an embarrassment or even a positive hindrance to the king.

The Franks had introduced their feudal usages into the conquered land. These met with no opposition from the natives who had long been accustomed to a somewhat similar régime and desired from their new masters only protection and a not too harsh rule. In the East the city had from antiquity been the most important center of government, as is evidenced by the city states. The Crusaders formed only a small part of the population in any city, even in Jerusalem. While the citadel built at one corner of the city was held by a garrison either Frankish or under the command of the Franks, the rest of the city was occupied by the natives, intent upon commerce and industry. The Franks respected the municipal institutions which they found and adopted them for the government of the cities. The Roman law was the basis of the jurisdiction. In each city the chief official was the viscount appointed by the Franks. Under the viscount was the mathesep (*muhtasib*) who had charge of policing the city, but the citizens had their own officials and managed their own affairs very much as they had done under former conquerors. Justice was administered under the viscount by native officials. Moreover, there was a conflict of authorities which turned to the advantage of the inhabitants and secured them many privileges. For example, in any large seaport there were usually: first, a Frankish noble, who held the city as a fief and defended it; second, a bishop who had jurisdiction over all cases which might be brought into the ecclesiastical courts and also held part of the property in the city as a feudal lord; third, one or more Italian consuls who exercised jurisdiction over the "quarters" which had been granted to the Italian cities for their support in capturing the land; lastly, the native officials whose actual powers were more extensive than any of the preceding in preserving order and controlling the daily activities of the citizens. Consequently the various western authorities vied with one another to obtain the good will of the natives and attract citizens to the parts of the cities under their control and thus to secure support and to increase their income.

The most important factor in the defense of the kingdom and the other states was the castles. These were usually situated where they controlled some caravan route or a pass between important cities. Thus the Crusaders were enabled to increase their income by levying tolls upon the commerce as well as to control the military roads and thus prevent sudden invasions. Especially important were the great fortresses beyond the Jordan which were situated along the caravan routes from Egypt to Damascus and the pilgrim road from Damascus to Mecca and Medina. The castles were most numerous in the north in the principality of Antioch and the county of Tripolis, because of the fact that Aleppo, Damascus, Hims, and Hamah, always held by the Muslims, might be sources of danger and also because the commerce between these cities and the coast cities was

TWO VIEWS OF KRAK DES CHEVALIERS, QALA'AT AL-HUSN

especially active. The best preserved castles are in the mountains north and northwest of Tripolis. Some of these were new foundations built by the Crusaders, others were of indefinite antiquity, as Shayzar, the home of Usamah. This never fell into the hands of the Christians.

One of the largest and the most famous of the castles was Krak of the Knights (Crac des Chevaliers) which was on a spur of the mountain and overlooked a narrow pass through which the caravans from Hims or Hamah went to Tripolis or Tortosa. The date of its building is entirely unknown, but probably there had been a castle at this point from a very early date, and the foundations of the present structure may be ancient. During the First Crusade the Franks had besieged Krak, which was then called the Castle of the Kurds, and, its defenders having fled, they had obtained great booty. Later it came into the possession of the Count of Tripolis and was given by him in 1145 to the Knights of the Hospital. Although damaged by an earthquake in 1170, it played an important part in the wars, especially in the time of Saladin. In time of peace Wilbrand of Oldenburg reports that it contained a garrison of two thousand. It is of great size, and the walls are almost intact today. The single entrance is a long narrow passage which could be defended easily. Inside are two enceintes, the upper one containing the *grande salle,* chapel, magazines, etc. There was an ample supply of water, both to fill the moat between the two enclosures and to supply the garrison, brought from a spring on a neighboring hill. This was only one of a chain of castles to defend the eastern frontiers of Tripolis.

Very few of the castles were held by the king; the defense of most was entrusted to the Templars or Hospitallers. Even those—like Karak beyond the Jordan—which were in lay hands, were in the possession of vassals who, as will be noted later, were often insubordinate.

Thus in spite of the ability and prowess of Baldwin I and Baldwin II, the wealth of the kingdom was not at the king's disposal, nor were the military forces which held the land.

CHAPTER V

RELATIONS BETWEEN CRUSADERS
AND NATIVES

THE Crusades were, in the words of Stevenson, "military expeditions to establish and maintain a Latin power in Syria." Long before, Kugler had written, "among those who have critically studied the history of the Middle Ages it is a recognized fact that the Crusades were to a great extent the result of economic causes and that they must be studied as a part of the general history of colonization."

To maintain their colonies and power the Crusaders needed the aid of the natives. While they received some supplies and money from the West and some aid from pilgrims, they had to depend wholly on the natives for labor to build the castles, to cultivate the soil, and to carry on the industries, for the Franks were comparatively few in number and were not as skillful as the natives in any of these kinds of work. The number of castles built in a few decades is astounding, and in addition earthquakes necessitated the rebuilding both of the castles the Crusaders had captured and of the new ones that they had built; for this the services of the natives, who were skilled architects, artists, and masons, were indispensable. As the methods of cultivation of the plants and fruits of Syria and Palestine were unknown to the Franks, they had to employ native farmers. The industries, such as dyeing and the manufacture of soap, glass, and pottery, for which Syria was famous, were carried on wholly by natives. In their frequent campaigns against the Muslims or against one another, they needed the services of the Maronite archers and of the skilled Armenian engineers. They also enrolled large numbers of Turcopoles, natives of mixed origin, who fought on horseback in native fashion. These formed a large portion of the forces of the Templars and Hospitallers as well as of the king's troops.

There was no unity, no common bond of religion or race among the inhabitants of Syria, and they had long been accustomed to submit to conquerors. Their chief anxiety was to be allowed to live without too much oppression or interference from their rulers. They were accustomed to a kind of feudal régime, too, and found the Frankish rule less burdensome in some respects than that of their former masters. This is brought out in a striking manner in the account given by Ibn-Jubayr, a Muslim from Spain, who on his return from a pilgrimage to Mecca passed through Syria in 1184. He says, "We left Tibnin (Toron) early Monday morning by a road which passed a continuous row of farms, wholly inhabited by Mussulmans, who live in great comfort under the Franks; may Allah preserve us from such a temptation! ... the Mussulmans are masters of their dwellings, and govern themselves as they wish. This is the case in all the territory occupied by the Franks upon the littoral of Syria, that is, of all the villages inhabited by the Mussulmans. The hearts of most Mussulmans are filled with the temptation of settling there, when they see the condition of their brethren in the districts governed by the Mussulmans, because the state of the latter is the reverse of comfortable.

"One of the misfortunes which afflict Mussulmans is that they have always reason for complaint, under their own government, of the injustice of their chiefs, and that they have cause only to praise the conduct of the Franks—and the justice on which one can always depend; but Allah is the only refuge for any one who complains of this state of affairs."

Ibn-Jubayr was not at all a lover or an admirer of the Franks. In speaking of Tibnin (Toron) he says: "It belongs to a sow (princess) known as the *queen,* and mother of this hog (king) of Acre—may Allah destroy him!" Elsewhere he writes: "Infidel cities are filthy, and the faithful have to go and come in the midst of pigs, and a whole host of other forbidden things which I could never finish enumerating. May we be preserved from entering the country of the infidels." For this reason his testimony is the more valuable, and his account of his stay in Syria is full of information as to the relations between the Crusaders and the Muslims.

A study of the administration and laws shows the care the Franks took to win the good will of the natives. The privileges granted to Syrians, Arabs, Greeks, and Armenians by Baldwin I and Baldwin

II have already been noted, as well as the self-government allowed to the native townspeople. The Syrians were at first allowed to have their own courts presided over by a native official. Later in the *cour de la fonde* a Frankish official, a *bailli,* presided, but of the six *jurés* who decided the cases, four were Syrians and two Franks. These courts had competence in commercial matters and in minor civil suits. "The native prejudices were recognized in the matter of oaths. The Mohammedan was permitted to swear on the Koran, the Jew on the Torah, the Samaritan on the books of the Pentateuch which he observed; Armenians, Syrians, and Greeks on the Cross. Moreover, a Saracen was permitted to clear himself of a charge of debt by such an oath if the accuser, who might even be a Frank, could not produce witnesses. In suits between people of different races or religions no one could be convicted except by witnesses of the same race as the accused. Thus a Frank, if he brought suit against a Syrian, must have Syrian witnesses to convict." [1] The Muslims testify that the Frankish courts were eminently fair; for example, Usamah tells of a law suit which he brought against a Frankish lord which was decided in his favor. The peasants, as described above by Ibn-Jubayr, praised the justice of the Franks, "on which one can always depend." Also, the peasants had to pay relatively slight dues: a corvée of one day's work each year was exacted from each plowland of about seventy-five acres; the

[1] F. Duncalf, in *Annual Report* of the American Historical Association for the Year 1914, Vol. I, p. 140.

share of the crop to be paid varied from one-quarter to one-half; occasionally there was a small poll tax. This was much less than was exacted by the Muslim lords (and it also compares favorably with the payments of the average tenant farmer at the present day, especially if all taxes are included). Consequently the natives were not unwilling to serve the Frankish conquerors.

Associations between them were inevitable, as was also intercourse between the Franks and the Mussulmans in the territory still unconquered. It will be remembered that the lands held by the Crusaders formed a narrow strip, usually not over fifty miles in width, extending from north to south, and that the Arabs always retained possession of the four cities, Aleppo, Hims, Hamah, and Damascus, as well as many another stronghold, such as Shayzar, the home of Usamah. No spot in the Christian territory was a day's ride from some land held by a potential enemy.

At the boundaries of the possessions of the two there was opportunity for friction which might lead to war. This is illustrated by Ibn-Jubayr's account. "When we had gone half the way, we came to an oak with an enormous trunk and large branches, which they told us was called 'the tree of the balance.' In response to our questions, they said that the name was given because the tree marked on this road the boundary between security and the danger of attack by Frankish brigands, i.e., either scouts or highwaymen. They seize as prisoners all whom they find beyond this tree on the Mussulman side, even if it is only by a span's distance; on the contrary, whosoever is beyond the tree on the Frankish side by the same distance can continue his journey in freedom. This regulation, which had been agreed upon, was observed strictly."

It was fortunate, probably, that the first contacts between Christians and Muslims had been in warfare, for the Crusaders had set out on their expedition with a contempt for their opponents. As reported by one chronicler, Pope Urban II said at Clermont: "For the Turk never ventures upon close fight; ... and as he has poisoned arrows, venom, and not valor, inflicts death on the man he strikes. Whatever he effects, then, I attribute to fortune, not to courage, because he wars by flight and poison. It is apparent, too, that every race, born in that region, being scorched with the intense heat of the sun, abounds more in reflection than in blood; and, therefore, they avoid coming to close quarters, because they are aware how little blood they possess." But when they fought together the Christians found that the Muslims were no cowards. One knight said if they had only been Christians "no one could find more powerful or braver, or more skillful warriors than they." Other Franks were equally emphatic. Raymond of Agiles writes, "Even if few in number they never hesitate to attack the enemy." Their skill and valor were also praised by Fulcher of Chartres, Ekkehard, and others. The Muslims, too, admired the bravery of the Franks; Nureddin said: "The Franks are the bravest of mortals." Usamah gave as his opinion that "the Franks are (may Allah curse them) the most prudent warriors in the world," and he meant by this the highest praise.

In their frequent battles many captives were taken and held for ransom. Bohemond, prince of Antioch, King Baldwin II, Count Raymond of Tripolis, and many another were long prisoners of the Muslims. Such captives seldom experienced harsh treatment, and usually no rancor seems to have been felt. Baldwin II, when a prisoner in Shayzar, was so kindly treated by the father and uncle of Usamah that he freed them from a tribute which they owed to the rulers of Antioch. The tales current in the West about the loves of Muslim princesses and Christian prisoners whom they freed from captivity are eloquent of this kindly treatment.

Both Christians and Muslims sought alliances with men of the other faith in their wars with their coreligionists. In 1108 Baldwin de Bourg, when besieged by. Tancred, was rescued by a Muslim ally. Because of their mutual fear of the Egyptian caliph the ruler of Damascus and the king of Jerusalem were for a long time in friendly relations. Examples of other alliances have already been mentioned and will be again. Both Muslim and Frankish princes maintained diplomatic agents at the various courts. Usamah mentions casually that "our representative" at the court of King Baldwin reported certain news. In 1169 Frankish consuls were even established at Cairo. Christian officials were stationed at Aleppo and Damascus to look after the interest of Christian slaves in those cities.

Commerce also brought the Franks and natives together. During the siege of Antioch, as has been mentioned, Armenian merchants from the city had sold provisions to the Crusaders, although at an exorbitant price. In 1099 the Christians had made "a firm peace with Ascalon on account of trade." In 1115 Baldwin I had allowed traders of all religions free entrance into Jerusalem. The following year Mohammedan caravans began again to go across the Christian territories because it was more convenient and the transit dues were small. Yet these tolls made up a considerable portion of the revenues of the king of Jerusalem.

The Christian seaports in Syria became active centers of trade. Muslim merchants had to pay a tax on their wares of one kirat per dinar of value (a dinar equals twenty-four kirats) when they entered Acre. This was the most important port. At Acre a strong trading company of men from Mosul lived under the protection of the Templars. In their bazaars could be found rich stuffs from Bagdad and Persia, glassware from 'Iraq, porcelain from China, pearls from the Persian Gulf, precious stones from India, ivory, perfumes, spices, and other wares from many a distant land, as well as the damascened bronzes for which Mosul was famous. There were two extremely wealthy merchants who were leading citizens of Damascus. "All their trade was carried on along the Frankish coast, where their names were held in high esteem and they had agents under their orders. Caravans which bore their merchandise were constantly going and coming; they had colossal fortunes, as well as great influence both with the Mussulman and Frankish princes." These native merchants were well received and well treated at Acre, according to the testimony of Ibn-Jubayr: "We were taken to the custom-house, a caravansary prepared to receive caravans. Before the gate is a carpeted platform, on which the Christian clerks sit. They have inkstands of ebony ornamented with gold-work. They keep their accounts in Arabic, and also speak this language. Their head, who is chief of the customs, is called simply *sahib*—a title derived from the importance of his work; for the Christians employ this name for all their important men who are not in the army. All the receipts belong to the chief of the custom-house, who pays a very large sum to the government. The merchants in our company carried their merchandise thither and installed themselves in the upper story. The baggage of those who had no merchandise was examined to make sure that it contained nothing dutiable, and then they were allowed to go where they pleased. The examination was made in a quiet and courteous manner, without any violence or overcharge."

Italian merchants from Venice, Pisa, and Genoa, and French from Marseilles, had their warehouses and caravansaries in the Syrian ports, and the Templars and Hospitallers also participated in the trade and had their own magazines. It was to the interest of these merchants and military orders that nothing should be done to offend the Muslim merchants or divert their trade. In addition to the exotic goods mentioned above Syria furnished many wares of its own manufacture, such as linen, silk, cotton, sugar, indigo, saffron, and the pottery for which Jaffa, Beirut, and Tyre were famous. In case of need Christians borrowed money from Muslims. Thus Baldwin II borrowed from Usamah's father, and the Orders of the Temple and Hospital had many dealings with the Muslims.

It could not be otherwise, for the people of the two religions mingled constantly. It is possible to trace such associations in the agreements made about hunting. Both Christians and Muslims were very fond of the chase, and they lived in such close proximity that it would have been impossible to have engaged in hunting if either party had been constantly exposed to the danger of being captured and held for ransom. Consequently hunting agreements were made which secured them against such a mischance. Rey states that "in the inventories of the archives of several Arab families in Syria there is mention of permissions to hunt granted, reciprocally, in certain limited portions of the two territories, by Christian princes and Persian emirs." The two at times met and hunted together. The Christians learned from the Muslims to use the cheetah, or hunting leopard, which afterwards became so popular with the rulers in the West. Each admired the other's falcons, dogs, and horses. Soon they began to trade these and this led to association. Thus Usamah says that there were "friendly relations and correspondence" between his father and the Armenian princes; the latter sent each year ten falcons, and his father sent in return horses, perfumes, and garments from Egypt.

In addition to hunting agreements, proximity led to many other associations. One of the most significant examples is given by Ibn-Jubayr: "In the neighboring plain there is a vast extent of cultivated land, dominated by a fort belonging to the Franks and named Honein. This is three parasangs from Paneas [Baniyas], the frontier town of the Mussulman territory. The district formed by this plain is shared equally by the Franks and the Mussulmans,—i.e., the two peoples divide into equal shares the crops which grow in it, and the herds of the two peoples pasture together without any wrong being done by either party."

"Safe conducts" were often obtained for travel. Thus Nureddin asked King Baldwin II to send him one so that Usamah and his family and goods might pass in safety from Egypt to Syria, either by land or sea. In this case the king caused the vessel to be wrecked so that he might profit by the right of flotsam and jetsam. Usamah lost property to the value of 30,000 dinars and his library of four thousand volumes. The king gave to the members of his family only 500 dinars for their expenses in returning home. Usually "safe conducts" were better respected, especially by the Muslims. They were given freely. Tancred wrote to the uncle of Usamah, "This is a revered knight of the Franks who has completed the holy pilgrimage and is now on his way back to his country. He has asked me to introduce him to you so that he may see your cavaliers. Accordingly, I have sent him to you. Treat him well." Roger of Antioch wrote to the uncle, saying, "I am dispatching one of my knights on urgent business to Jerusalem, and I ask thee to send an escort of horsemen to take him from Afamiyah and conduct him to Rafaniyah." These examples illustrate the prevalence of such passports.

Contacts and mutual respect led to many friendships. Baldwin I had shown great courtesy to the wife of one of the shaykhs whom he had captured in 1101 in his expedition across the Jordan. He liberated her, and her husband became one of the most faithful allies of the Franks. The friendship of Raymond of Tripolis and Saladin will be recorded later. Usamah writes, "In the army of King Fulk, son of Fulk, was a Frankish reverend knight who had just arrived from their land in order to make the holy pilgrimage and then return home. He was of my intimate fellowship and kept such constant company with me that he began to call me 'my brother.' Between us were mutual bonds of amity and friendship. When he resolved to return by sea to his homeland, he said to me: 'My brother, I am leaving for my country and I want thee to send with me thy son (my son, who was then fourteen years old, was at that time in my company) to our country, where he can see the knights and learn wisdom and chivalry. When he returns, he will be like a wise man.' Thus there fell upon my ears words which would never come out of the head of a sensible man; for even if my son were to be taken captive, his captivity could not bring him a worse misfortune than carrying him into the lands of the Franks. However, I said to the man: 'By thy life, this has exactly been my idea. But the only thing that prevented me from carrying it out was the fact that his grandmother, my mother, is so fond of him and did not this time let him come out with me until she exacted an oath from me to the effect that I would return him to her.' Thereupon he asked, 'Is thy mother still alive?' 'Yes,' I replied. 'Well,' said he, 'disobey her not.'" Actual compacts of brotherhood were entered into between Muslims and Christians. Count Joscelin gave up some booty which he had captured when he learned that it belonged to a Muslim with whom he had such a compact.

Courtesies were frequently exchanged, and examples will be cited later in connection with Saladin's career. Christian rulers frequently sought the loan of physicians from Muslim rulers, as the skill of the eastern doctors was highly appreciated by the Franks. When King Amalric saw that his son, later King Baldwin the Leper, was suffering from a disease which the Christian doctors could not diagnose, he sought the services of the most skillful doctors in Damascus. An amusing illustration of the difference in methods between the doctors of the West and of the Orient is given in the naïve account of a Muslim physician who had been loaned to a Frankish lord to treat some difficult cases: "They brought before me a knight in whose leg an abscess had grown; and a woman afflicted with imbecility. To the knight I applied a small poultice until the abscess opened and became well; and the woman I put on a diet and made her humor wet. Then a Frankish physician came to them and said, 'This man knows nothing about treating them.' He then said to the knight, 'Which wouldst thou prefer, living with one leg or dying with two?' The latter replied, 'Living with one leg.' The physician said, 'Bring me a strong knight and a sharp ax.' A knight came with the ax. And I was standing by. Then the physician laid the leg of the patient on a block of wood and bade the knight strike his leg with the ax and chop it off at one blow. Accordingly he struck it—while I was looking on—one blow, but the leg was not severed. He dealt another blow, upon which the marrow of the leg flowed out and the patient died on the spot. He then examined the woman and said, 'This is a woman in whose head there is a devil which has possessed her. Shave off her hair.' Accordingly they shaved it off, and the woman began once more to eat their ordinary diet—garlic and mustard. Her imbecility took a turn for the worse. The physician then said, 'The devil has penetrated through her head.' He therefore took a razor, made a deep cruciform incision on it, peeled off the skin at the middle of the incision until the bone of the skull was exposed and rubbed it with salt. The woman also expired instantly. Thereupon I asked them whether my services were needed any longer, and when they replied in the negative I returned home, having learned of their medicine what I knew not before."

The most intimate associations naturally resulted from marriages. All classes from the highest to the lowest felt no aversion to such unions. Of the kings, Baldwin I and Baldwin II married Armenians. Baldwin III and Amalric I married Greek princesses. The movement was a reciprocal one. Emperor Manuel married Mary of Antioch, and later, the favorite wife of Sultan Baybars was a Christian. The common people entered into such marriages from the very first. Usamah tells of several marriages between Muslims and Christian captives. "A number of maids taken captive from the Franks were brought into the home of my father (may Allah's mercy rest upon his soul!). The Franks (may Allah's curse be upon them!) are an accursed race, the members of which do not assimilate except with their own kin. My father saw among them a pretty maid who was in the prime of youth, and said to his housekeeper, 'Introduce this woman into the bath, repair her clothing, and prepare her for a journey.' This she did. He then delivered the maid to a servant of his and sent her to al-Amir Shihab-al-Din Malik ibn-Salim, the lord of the Castle of Ja'bar, who was a friend of his. He also wrote him a letter, saying, 'We have won some booty from the Franks, from which I am sending thee a share.' The maid suited Shihab-al-Din, and he was pleased with her. He took her to himself and she bore him a boy, whom he called Badran. Badran's father named him his heir apparent, and he became of age. On his father's death, Badran became the governor of the town and its people, his mother being the real power. She entered into conspiracy with a band of men and let herself down from the castle by a rope. The band took her to Saruj, which belonged at that time to the Franks. There she married a Frankish shoemaker, while her son was the lord of the Castle of Ja'bar."

The offspring of the marriages between Franks and natives were very numerous and, while somewhat despised by the Franks, were the most potent intermediaries in causing the adoption of native customs. "Their children, who are called Pullani, were brought up in luxury, soft and effeminate, more used to baths than battles, addicted to unclean and riotous living, clad like women in soft robes, and ornamented even as the polished corners of the Temple; how slow and slothful, how timid and cowardly they proved themselves against the enemies of Christ, is doubted by no one who knows how greatly they are despised by the Saracens. A multitude of Saracens would flee from before their fathers, even though they were few; at the voice of their thunder they hasted away; but they feared their cowardly descendants no more than so many women, unless they had some French or other Westerns with them." The Pullani conformed so closely to Muslim usages as to excite the wrath of zealous churchmen. "They are suspicious and jealous of their wives, whom they lock up in close prison, and guard in such strict and careful custody that even their brethren and nearest relatives can scarce come at them; while they forbid them so utterly to attend churches, processions, the wholesome preaching of God's Word, and other matters appertaining to their salvation, that they scarce suffer them to go to church once a year; howbeit some husbands allow their wives to go out to the bath three times a week, under strict guard. The richest and most powerful of them, to show that they are Christians, and to somewhat excuse their conduct, cause altars to be set up near their wives' beds, and get Masses performed by starveling chaplains and half-fledged priests." As the Pullani made their living by catering to the wants of the pilgrims, they got a very bad reputation; they were accused of outrageous charges to the pilgrims for lodging and other services, of cheating and plundering, and of pouring contempt upon the "warriors and exiles for Christ's sake, insulting them and calling them the idiots," but their services were much in demand, and they exercised a great influence on the habits of the other Franks.

The Franks relished the luxuries and food with which they became acquainted in Syria. The use of spices became universal and soon spread to the West. The castors, which are now sought by collectors of antiques, were adopted from the Muslims to hold the various spices desired on every table. Persian wines and drinks cooled with snow from Lebanon or Hermon became popular. The Christians also learned to avoid eating pork, and Muslim guests at table were assured that they would find no food forbidden to them by the Koran.

The Franks admired and wore the flowing garments and the turbans. They allowed their beards to grow in imitation of the Muslims. Furred robes and shoes with long curved points became fashionable. The Arabic kufiyah was worn over the Western helmet to ward off the heat of the sun. Its common use is shown by the fact that it became the origin of the heraldic lambrequin. The churches were built in Western style, but decorated by Greek or Saracen artists. The castles, as has been noted, were much influenced by those that the Crusaders found in Syria. Houses were seized from the natives, and when new ones were built these were copies of the oriental models, and were supplied with running water, fountains, glass windows, perfumed candles; the walls were adorned with hangings, porcelains, and bronzes. At the banquets the Christians employed Saracen entertainers and dancing girls; in the baths, Saracen attendants; for funerals they hired professional mourners, as did the Muslims. The streets of Tyre and Acre were hung with stuffs, as in the days of Muslim rule.

In order to carry on commerce with the Muslims and other natives, the Christians had to adopt the weights and measures in use in the country and needed a form of money which would be acceptable to the Oriental merchants. While Greek and western coins were used among the Crusaders, a new coin, the saracenate, or bezant, or dinar of Tyre, was struck for use in commerce. This was a gold coin imitating closely the standard bezant, coined by Muslims, with

Arabic legend, usually a text from the Koran. This became the coin commonest in use in the land of Outre-Mer, and references to it are very frequent in the documents. It is interesting to note that it continued to be used by the Crusaders till the visit of St. Louis to the Holy Land in the middle of the thirteenth century. Then Pope Innocent IV forbade such impiety, and through the influence of Louis the texts from the Koran were replaced on the coin by Christian inscriptions, but these were still written in Arabic in order not to prevent the circulation of the coins among the Muslims.[2] Commerce was bound by no religious or racial scruples.

The kingship took on an oriental character. The king was approached humbly with bent knee. He made a royal progress through the streets, surrounded by pompous escorts; at home he sat with crossed legs encased in purple boots, in Muslim fashion, on rich rugs. What a change for the rude western warriors! For attendants in the palaces, eunuchs were employed.

Ideas changed rapidly, even in regard to religious matters. Sybel attributes the decline of the kingdom of Jerusalem to the loss of religious zeal. This was

[2] Similar devices to insure circulation of coins among peoples of other faiths were not uncommon. In the Spanish peninsula Christian rulers had minted coins with Arabic legends. Some Muslims adopted a similar device, and "on coins of the Urtukis, for example, a petty dynasty of some crusading fame that ruled a few fortresses in Mesopotamia, we meet with not only the figures of Byzantine emperors, but those of Christ and the Virgin, with mangled inscriptions of Christian import. Figures of a similar character also appear on the coinage of the Ayyubis (Saladin's Kurdish house), and that of the Beny Zangy of Mosul and Syria, together with the earliest known representation of the two-headed eagle, which has since obtained high favor in Europe."

brought about by the admiration felt for the Muslims
and by the constant associations with men of so many
different sects. They all met at common shrines. In
the Church of the Holy Sepulchre, as today, different
Christian sects worshipped; but the intermingling at
holy places was not confined to Christians. At the
great cathedral of Tortosa both Christians and Muslims worshipped. The fig tree, which had furnished
food for the Virgin Mary, the spring where she had
washed the Infant's clothes, were reverenced by the
followers of both religions. The chapel built near
the Burning Bush seen by Moses was entered by
Muslims barefooted, as in their own mosques. Muslim parents brought their children to Christian
priests to be baptized, because they thought that this
would make them stronger and more healthy. Our
Lady of Sardenay, in a village northwest of Damascus,
worked miracles for Muslims as well as Christians;
by her intervention a sultan of Damascus was healed
of his blindness. Ibn-Jubayr says: "In the eastern
part of the city of Acre is the Spring of the Ox. From
this Allah caused the ox to come forth for Adam.
The descent to the spring is by polished steps. Near
this spring there was formerly a mosque, of which
the oratory remained uninjured. To the east of it
the Franks have constructed an oratory; thus, Mussulmans and infidels meet there—although it belongs to
the Christians—and each one says his prayers, facing
in the direction that his faith prescribes." In the
Christian cities mosques were set apart for the use
of the faithful. "Whenever I visited Jerusalem,"

INTERIOR OF THE CHURCH OF NOTRE DAME AT TORTOSA
(TARTUS)

Usamah writes, "I always entered the Aqsa Mosque, beside which stood a small mosque which the Franks had converted into a church. When I used to enter the Aqsa Mosque, which was occupied by the Templars, who were my friends, the Templars would evacuate the little adjoining mosque so that I might pray in it. One day I entered this mosque, repeated the first formula, 'Allah is great,' and stood up in the act of praying, upon which one of the Franks rushed on me, got hold of me and turned my face eastward saying, 'This is the way thou shouldst pray!' A group of Templars hastened to him, seized him and repelled him from me. I resumed my prayer. The same man, while the others were otherwise busy, rushed once more on me and turned my face eastward, saying, 'This is the way thou shouldst pray!' The Templars again came in to him and expelled him. They apologized to me, saying, 'This is a stranger who has only recently arrived from the land of the Franks and he has never before seen anyone praying except eastward.' Thereupon I said to myself, 'I have had enough prayer.' So I went out and have ever been surprised at the conduct of this devil of a man, at the change in the color of his face, his trembling, and his sentiment at the sight of one praying towards the *qiblah*."

There were many attempts, some partially successful, at a union of various Christian sects. Among the suffragans of the Latin patriarch of Jerusalem were the Armenian archbishop and the Jacobite bishop. Many Greeks recognized the supremacy of the Latin hierarchy, and there were some conversions from

Islam to Christianity, but one of the churchmen writes sorrowfully that he "fears these are not genuine, but induced by fear or interest." Franks became renegades to the Christian religion in times of peril, or when compelled because of their crimes to flee from justice. Some of these converts to Islam secured high positions at the courts of Saracen rulers and had no incentive to return to their co-religionists.

The Christian attitude toward the Jews in the Holy Land was not as favorable as toward the Muslims. While the Jews had the rights of citizenship and a good position legally, their witness being received in court as equal to that of the Christians, they were not permitted to hold land. There were evidently intermarriages between Jews and Christians, as such marriages were repeatedly denounced by zealous clerics, who also warned against the employment of Jewish doctors in Christian families. When Benjamin of Tudela, our chief authority, travelled through the country shortly before the Third Crusade, there were only a few thousand Jews in all the Christian territories; not as many as were to be found in the two cities of Damascus and Ba'labakk. Benjamin mentions few outstanding Jews living among the Franks, but he found many more at Damascus.

Muslim writers frequently praised Christian leaders such as Joscelin, who in the words of Kemaleddin "made himself famous for his generosity and courage." Christian writers, although mainly of the clergy, admitted the good points of an adversary. Thus

Bishop William of Tyre characterized Nureddin as "the greatest persecutor of the Christian name and faith, nevertheless a just prince."

It is significant that Christians soon came to boast of Muslim descent. The change in their point of view can be gathered from two legends. The first explained the greatness of Zangi by giving him as his mother Countess Ida of Austria, and the second explained Thomas Becket's remarkable ability by giving him a Saracen mother. Such feelings of mutual admiration were confined, as might be expected, to the leading men of either faith; the lower classes, as Ibn-Jubayr says, "heap curses on Mohammed, whom Allah has exalted." The Muslims noted that the streets and lanes of Tyre were cleaner than those of Acre, the infidel belief of its inhabitants of a more courteous character, and their habits and feelings more generous towards Mussulmans.

As these quotations indicate, good feelings between Franks and natives were by no means universal. In fact, in reading the western chronicles of the Crusades a very different impression is formed. The writers, almost all of whom were members of the clergy, were opposed to the tendencies springing up in the Holy Land, and spoke of the natives as "people odious to the Divinity." Few of them were residents in the Holy Land, and newcomers were by no means as tolerant as those Christians who had spent years in the land. Usamah noted that "everyone who is a fresh emigrant from the Frankish lands is ruder in character than those who have become acclimatized and have held long association with the Moslems."

Adventurers who were out to achieve fortune by fighting were as biased as the clerical writers and had an attitude entirely different from that of the Italian or French merchants, who preferred peaceful associations with the natives.[3] Finally it must be noted that the Muslim writers frequently felt a certain amount of contempt for the western barbarians, especially for some of their customs. It is easy to understand such contempt when one reads Usamah's account of a wager of battle, or of an ordeal, or of the race for the pig on the part of two old women; this last delighted the Frankish nobles who had arranged it and who laughed when the old women fell down. No Muslim gentleman could find any amusement in such mockery of old women.

[3] Jacques de Vitry thus describes the Italians: "The Italians are graver and more discreet, prudent and wary, frugal in eating, sober in drinking. They make long and polished speeches, are wise in their counsels, eager and zealous to further the interests of their own States, grasping and provident for the future. . . . They are very necessary to the Holy Land, not only for fighting, but for seafaring, and carrying merchandise, pilgrims, and victuals. As they are sparing of food and drink, they live longer in the East than other nations of the West."

CHAPTER VI

THE DECLINE OF THE KINGDOM

THE kingdom of Jerusalem had reached maturity
under Baldwin II. As he had no son, he asked the
king of France to suggest a suitable husband for his
oldest daughter, to be his successor. King Louis suggested Fulk, count of Anjou, who had been a
Templar for a time and was much interested in the
fortunes of the kingdom of Jerusalem. The choice
seemed a happy one, and Fulk was married to the
heiress, for the kingdom, like the fiefs in Jerusalem,
was to become hereditary. The character of the feudal
kingdom and the ascendency of the monarchy is
definitely shown by the fact that Fulk was crowned
in the Church of the Holy Sepulchre. Even Baldwin
II, like Baldwin I, had been crowned at Bethlehem.

At the time of his marriage Fulk was about thirty-
seven years old, and had won a high reputation for
ability both in the West and in the Holy Land, to
which he had made a pilgrimage about 1120. But he
was confronted with a difficult task as king, because,
as Ibn-al-Athir notes under the year 1132, strife between the Frankish rulers in Syria had become
habitual. Fulk had to put down a rebellion within
his kingdom, to fight against the count of Tripolis,
and repeatedly to thwart the machinations of his

sister-in-law at Antioch, as well as to ward off attacks from the Muslims. He fought vigorously against all obstacles; the tales, repeated after William of Tyre, about his weakness, uxoriousness, and feeble memory are untrue. When he died as the result of a fall while hunting, he was still a vigorous man in the early fifties. He left two sons, Baldwin III, thirteen years of age, and Amalric, seven, and his widow, who was crowned jointly with her oldest son to look after the rule of the kingdom.

During Fulk's reign, conditions among the Muslims had changed. During the first three decades of Frankish rule in Syria, there had been no great leader and no unity among their foes; the Christians had had to fight only against individual Turkish chiefs who were generally at strife with the neighboring Turkish rulers.

In 1128, however, when the fortunes of Islam seemed at their lowest ebb a champion appeared to fight its battles. This was Zangi, a brave, blue-eyed Turk. It happened that the ruler of Mosul had died, leaving only a young lad as his heir, and the boy's guardians sought for some one strong enough to defend Mosul until the heir should come of age. They sent messengers to the sultan at Bagdad to secure the recognition of the young prince's right to inherit Mosul, and the nomination of a regent. Their attention was called to Zangi by some of his friends, and they asked the sultan to appoint him as regent. He was then about forty-three years old. When he was only ten he had lost his father, and since that time had served under various lords, taking part in many battles against the Crusaders. He seemed suitable for the position and was appointed by the sultan as atabek, or lieutenant, to the ruler of Mosul. He never sought a higher title.

Zangi found the greater part of the city of Mosul in ruins and the government too weak to maintain order. His strong rule gave security and attracted many to settle in the city; he strengthened its walls, deepened the moat, and beautified the city. He caused gardens to be planted about it, so that fruits which had been scarce and expensive became abundant and cheap. He made a truce with the Christian ruler of Edessa and thus was free to devote his efforts to the conquest of his Muslim neighbors. He rewarded his followers liberally, giving fiefs to the officers, but not allowing them to buy land, as he wished them to be wholly dependent upon him. He was entirely unscrupulous in his methods, employing wiles and treachery to aid his armies. He maintained a corps of spies who reported to him all that was done at Bagdad or at the courts of his Muslim and Christian neighbors. His men were devoted to him, but stood in terror of his strict justice and stern rule. He punished insults to women, and especially to the wives of his soldiers, with the utmost severity. When he learned that one of his most trusted officers, whom he had placed in command of a city, was leading a licentious life, Zangi sent another official with orders to mutilate him and tear out his eyes, so that he might be punished in the two members in which he had sinned, and then to crucify him. But in order to secure the offender's wealth and to prevent any attempt at rescue by his followers, the criminal was to be told that Zangi had promoted him to a higher office. Suspecting nothing, he got together all his moveable wealth and set out under the conduct of the official, who carried out the sentence. In this way Zangi secured all the criminal's wealth.

He captured Aleppo from his Muslim neighbors in 1128 and Hamah in 1129. Then taking advantage of the civil strife in Antioch, he took from the Christians several cities, of which Ma'arrah was the most important. The Franks had captured this city in 1098 and confiscated all the land. When Zangi recaptured the city the former landowners, or their heirs, requested the return of their lands. Zangi asked to see their title deeds, and they replied that the Franks had burned them. Then Zangi had the records at Aleppo searched, and wherever the records showed that an inhabitant of Ma'arrah had been assessed for a tax the property was returned to him or to his heirs.

Zangi was hated by the sultan at Bagdad, his overlord, and by his Muslim neighbors, but he had become the champion of Islam against the Christians, and he was followed blindly by his own men. He exacted very heavy taxes on the ground that he was using the income to fight the Christians. When the Greek emperor Manuel joined with the Franks to attack Aleppo, his position seemed desperate, and he sent to Bagdad to ask the sultan to send an army to his rescue. The sultan refused. Then Zangi's agents in Bagdad stirred up riots among the riffraff of the population who interrupted the services in the mosques and threatened the sultan's life. The sultan had to agree to send troops to aid in the Holy War; but their presence was not needed, and they were allowed to return home before reaching Aleppo, for Zangi had succeeded in stirring up dissensions between the Greeks and the Franks so that they had abandoned the siege.

In 1144 Zangi felt strong enough to attack Edessa. By a stratagem he induced the unsuspecting count to leave the city with his troops. Then he attacked. Edessa was defended with desperate valor by its bishop and inhabitants, but in vain. The skillful Aleppan sappers undermined the walls, the city was captured, and for three hours there was an indiscriminate slaughter of men, women, and children. Then Zangi checked it and, while the few Franks in the city were put to death, the Armenian and Syrian inhabitants were spared and their property restored to them. A garrison was left to defend the town, and the people were allowed to continue their peaceful pursuits. The news of the capture of Edessa delighted the Muslims and miraculous tales spread concerning it. It gave new courage to Islam; Zangi's fame increased.

Two years later Zangi was assassinated in his sleep by one of his followers. His assassin was a trusted retainer who either bore him a secret grudge or, as another account has it, feared the severe punishment with which Zangi had threatened him for some mis-

deed. The murderer—who was reported to have
been of Frankish origin—took advantage of Zangi's
drunken sleep, and, with the connivance and assistance of certain of his comrades, assassinated the
atabek in spite of the armed guard about his tent.

He was succeeded by two sons, one of whom,
Nureddin, became atabek of Aleppo and the pro-
tagonist of the Muslims in their conflict against the
Christians. He was then twenty-eight years of age.
He became noted as "a great builder, a great patron
of science and letters," but above all for his religious
zeal in combating the Franks. His first task was to
recapture Edessa; for on the news of the death of
Zangi, Joscelyn, the former ruler, had entered into
communication with its inhabitants and then entered
the city with some troops, but the Turkish garrison
held out in the citadel. While he was besieging the
latter, Nureddin came with an army of 10,000.
Joscelyn evacuated the city in the night, and the
inhabitants, fearing the vengeance of the Turks, went
with him. The Turks pursued, put the Frankish
knights to flight and slaughtered the foot-soldiers and
people. When they were finally weary of the slaughter
they tied up all the remainder in long lines and compelled them to follow, on foot, their Turkish masters
on horseback. The number of the slaves whom they
carried off was between twelve and sixteen thousand,
mainly young women and children. Thirty thousand
people had perished in the two slaughters, and Edessa
was left uninhabited, to become the home of wild
beasts.

A little later Nureddin was the ally of the count of Tripolis in one of his wars against fellow-Christians. In 1154 he obtained Damascus, mainly by his cunning, but partly because the inhabitants were dissatisfied with their leader and preferred Nureddin, who had a reputation among the Muslims for bravery, justice, piety, and good government. He then had virtually all the Muslims in Syria under his leadership and could count upon some aid from Mesopotamia. Fortunately for the Crusaders, his attention was directed mainly against the Muslims of Egypt.

The news of the fall of Edessa was followed by the Second Crusade. On December 1, 1145, Pope Eugene III issued a bull directed especially to the French urging them to emulate the virtues of their ancestors and offering the same privileges as had Urban II. Without entering into much disputed questions, it may be said that the real beginning of the Crusade was the declaration by Louis VII that he planned to take the Cross. He was moved by his desire to atone for the burning of Christians in the church at Vitry in 1142, and also by the fact that he had inherited the vow made by his brother to go on a Crusade. His nobles held back until Bernard of Clairvaux, at the pope's command, lent the weight of his mighty eloquence to preach the Crusade at Vézelay. His success was wonderful. As he wrote to the pope, "You have commanded, I have obeyed. Because of my preaching, towns and castles are empty of inhabitants, seven women can scarcely find one man.... Everywhere widows remain behind, while husbands are still alive." It would have been well for the success of the Crusade if this had been more strictly true; many women went, and Eleanor of Aquitaine, who accompanied her husband, King Louis, was the cause of much trouble and scandal.

The German emperor, Conrad III, who had already made a pilgrimage to Jerusalem, was moved by the eloquence of Bernard and also took the Cross. An army of Germans which included Frederick Barbarossa set out under his leadership. But the expedition was an entire failure. The Greeks were accused of treachery, and the Turks destroyed or enslaved many pilgrims in Asia Minor. Only a small part of the great hosts reached Jerusalem. An attack upon Damascus was agreed upon by the two kings and the nobles of Palestine, but this was frustrated by the treachery of some of the latter, and Louis and Conrad returned home bitterly incensed. Bernard wrote in his sorrow: "We have fallen on evil days, in which the Lord, provoked by our sins, has judged the world, with justice indeed, but not with his wonted mercy.... The sons of the Church have been overthrown in the desert, slain with the sword, or destroyed by famine. We promised good things, and behold, disorder! The judgments of the Lord are righteous, but this one is an abyss so deep that I must call him blessed who is not scandalised therein."

Popular feeling was also very strong. In Asia Minor many a pilgrim, it is reported, became a renegade to the Christian faith because of the good treatment received from the Muslims. It was also reported that the common people said it was not necessary to capture cities for the Crusaders because the Turks are better and more trustworthy than they who keep no faith to God or duty to neighbor.

Probably the Greek emperor was pleased at the failure of this Crusade. John and Manuel had continued the policy of Alexius and wished to reconquer Antioch and other lands near the Euphrates which had been captured by Turks, Armenians, or Latins. Fortunately for the Franks in the Holy Land, the Greeks were much hindered by wars against the Hungarians, Serbs, and Normans, and especially by their attempts to reconquer Asia Minor, which kept them from employing their strength in Syria and Palestine.

They made repeated attempts to secure Antioch by marriage with an heiress, and they always insisted upon their claims to the overlordship of the city because of the treaty of 1108. Prince Raymond was compelled to take an oath of fealty to the Greek emperor, John, and in 1138 the latter entered Antioch and demanded the citadel. A riot, cleverly fomented by Raymond, forced him to leave the city, and his later attempt was foiled by his death in 1143. Manuel, who succeeded him, was determined to have his authority recognized over the Latin rulers, and eventually succeeded, but he was constantly hindered by his wars against various Muslims, with whom, however, he was sometimes in alliance, and by the ambitions of the Armenian and Latin princes who were nominally his vassals, but always ready to seize an opportunity to attack Greek possessions.

In the face of all these dangers the Christians did not work together. The rulers of the principalities engaged in strife with one another and frequently called in Muslim allies to aid them in their wars against their fellow-Christians. In the kingdom the vassals were becoming less subordinate, and the patriarch was intent upon asserting his power. The military orders which had begun so humbly had gained great wealth and had become bitter rivals. They were the real military strength of the Franks and were constantly recruited from knights, especially from France. Many of the most important castles were given to them to defend. Their wealth became enormous; their commercial and trading activities will be noted later. It is symptomatic of the age that the Assassins became tributary to the Templars in 1152, and a little later in the century passed under the power of the Knights of the Hospital. Each order exploited them for its own advantage.

The authority of the rulers was still further limited by the privileges and lands which were in the hands of the Italian cities. Long before the Crusades began, Amalfi had had a colony at Jerusalem and another at Antioch for the purpose of carrying on trade with the Arabs. From their colony at Jerusalem had sprung first the Nursing Brotherhood, and later the order of the Knights of the Hospital. They also obtained quarters in Tripolis and Acre. All of these were the properties of the archbishop of Amalfi and were administered by the Amalfitans in the East.

By the treaty of 1123 the Venetians had been given

a quarter in every city of the kingdom. These were all under the control of the Venetian noble appointed by the Grand Consul, and all Venetians in Syria took an oath of fealty to him. In addition, Genoa and Pisa had extensive quarters in various cities under the control of their consuls. In connection with their quarters in the cities they also held agricultural domains, from which they derived food and income. Thus the resources and powers of the rulers were still further diminished.

Although the Italians were obliged to aid in guarding the cities in which they held properties, their participation in military undertakings was wholly voluntary and was frequently refused. They, as well as the military orders, were free from the jurisdiction of the patriarch and thus ecclesiastical unity was also lacking. Moreover, their interests were frequently antagonistic to the interests of the Frankish authorities, as the last thing they desired was a continuous war with the Muslims, which would have ruined commerce.

Very different was the attitude of the adventurers who flocked to the Holy Land to carve out their fortunes. They were eager to fight and win booty. One of the most interesting of the adventurers was Reginald of Chatillon, who went on the Second Crusade with Louis VII, and later entered the service of Raymond, prince of Antioch. The latter died in 1149 leaving a widow, Constance, and four children, the oldest only about five. King Baldwin III of Jerusalem had to take the guardianship of the principality, and Reginald remained in his service at Antioch. The king was anxious to be relieved of the burden of the distant principality and urged Constance, who was only twenty-two, to marry again. She had been married to Raymond when she was nine or ten years old. Her hand was sought by many suitors, among them two Greek princes, but she refused them all. Before her first marriage, when she was a mere child, she had been suggested as the wife of the emperor of Constantinople's heir, who was later the Emperor Manuel, but the Greek emperor had refused. This embittered the relations between the latter and the princes of Antioch. It is interesting to note that one of Constance's daughters later married Manuel, who had refused Constance, and the other married one of the suitors whom her mother had rejected.

The young widow was difficult to please, but in 1153 she fell in love with Reginald, who was young and brave and handsome. The king gladly consented to their marriage, as he wished to be freed from the burden of the guardianship. The patriarch at Antioch who had opposed the marriage and antagonized Reginald was imprisoned by him. In the words of William of Tyre, Reginald committed "a still greater deviltry." For he had the patriarch scourged and then bound naked on the highest tower, after smearing honey on his bald head and the wounds made by the scourge. The prelate was left there all day in the broiling sun, tortured by the insects. One of the Byzantine historians says that Reginald did this to extort the patriarch's wealth. The king of Jerusalem interfered and ordered Reginald to release the patriarch, who went to Jerusalem to live.

Soon after this Reginald made war upon Thoros, the ruler of Armenia, probably successfully, although the chroniclers give contradictory statements. At all events the war was a short one, and the two were soon in alliance, for the Greek emperor had promised to help pay Reginald's expenses in fighting the Armenians and did not keep his word. Consequently Reginald made an expedition against Cyprus. The island, which belonged to the Greek Empire, was very wealthy, and it had only a small garrison, as no attack was expected. Reginald's troops were veritable brigands whom he had gathered for the expedition, and they delighted in torturing the people. The whole island was sacked, villages were burned, convents plundered, fruit trees wantonly destroyed. The brigands raged especially against the priests and monks, cutting off hands, feet, ears, or noses. Many of the wealthiest inhabitants and high church officials were carried off by Reginald and held for ransom. William of Tyre says that Reginald returned to Antioch immensely enriched but cursed not only by the Greeks but also by the Latins who up to that time had lived in harmony with the Cypriots.

Naturally the Greek emperor was very angry, but he had to wait more than two years before he could proceed against Reginald. Then with a great army he approached Antioch. Reginald realized that resistance was impossible and humbly begged for pardon.

After negotiations to insure his safety, he presented himself before the emperor, bareheaded and barefooted, with his sleeves drawn up to his elbows and with a hangman's rope around his neck, accompanied by a long train of the principal personages in his principality and many monks. The emperor was seated on a throne. Reginald had to prostrate himself in the dust and lay there, as William of Tyre says, "crying for mercy, and he cried so long that everyone was nauseated and many of the Franks despised him and blamed him." Ambassadors from many oriental lands were present as witnesses of this humiliation. Finally the emperor deigned to pardon him.

The attack on Cyprus and the humiliation were only episodes in Reginald's life as prince of Antioch. Most of his time was spent in warring against the Muslims; he was always clad in armor and never wore silks or furs. He was much dreaded by the Muslims, and great was their joy at his capture in 1160, when although there was a truce between the Muslims and Christians, Reginald, hearing of an opportunity to get rich booty, had made a raid into the territory of Nureddin. Hampered by the booty which they were carrying off, Reginald and his followers were overcome, in spite of Reginald's prowess, and he was stripped of his clothes, tied upon a camel, and carried to Aleppo. He remained a prisoner for sixteen years, before his friends were able to raise the enormous ransom which was demanded for him.

Then he returned to Antioch. His wife had died; his stepson was ruling and there was no place for him. He went to Jerusalem. The king, glad to have the services of so brave a warrior, gave him in marriage the heiress of the fief beyond the Jordan. This consisted mainly of castles which had been built along the caravan routes which went from Damascus to Egypt and Mecca. The strongest castles were Karak and Montreal, which protected the frontier of the Frankish kingdom. His wife, like most of the noble heiresses in the kingdom of Jerusalem who married very young and before they were thirty frequently had two or three husbands and two or three sets of children, had been married twice before and had had two children by her first husband, one of whom was to marry the sister of the king of Jerusalem and the other the ruler of Armenia. It was a noticeable fact that the women of Frankish nationality were usually longer-lived in the Holy Land than their husbands.[1]

Reginald's new fief was a very important one because it guarded the confines of the kingdom beyond the Dead Sea and possessed a large income

---

[1] E.g., Isabel, the second daughter of Amalric and Maria Comnena, married (at 11) Humphrey of Toron, but was separated from him after several years of marriage and married Conrad of Montferrat. He had already had two wives, and it is not certain that his last wife was either dead or divorced. When he was murdered by an assassin, Isabel within a week married Henry of Champagne, who died in 1198, and then Amalric II of Cyprus. Agnes, daughter of Joscelyn II, married first Raynald of Marasch, who died in 1149; after having been betrothed to Hugh of Ibelin, she next married Amalric, king of Jerusalem, and had two children, Baldwin IV, and Sibyl. In 1162 Amalric divorced her on the ground of consanguinity, but really as a condition of receiving the crown. She then married Hugh of Ibelin and afterwards Reginald of Sidon, and again was divorced on account of consanguinity. Later she was reported to have been the mistress of the patriarch of Jerusalem.

from the tolls levied upon the caravans which passed by its castles. Reginald added to this income by occasionally plundering a caravan. The fief included Hebron on the west of the Jordan, and extended to the Red Sea, and the peninsula of Sinai was also under its jurisdiction; it owed the king the service of sixty knights. In addition to the tolls levied on the caravans there was an income from the rich harvests of the land of Moab and from the dues levied on all vessels on the Dead Sea. The fief had gradually become almost independent of the king and needed the services of an indefatigable warrior like Reginald. Unfortunately he soon showed that he was careless of the general interests of the kingdom and would not observe any truce when there was a chance of booty.

His most noted exploit was an attempt to sack Mecca and Medina, the holy cities of the Muslims. As the only port which the Christians had possessed on the Red Sea had been recaptured by the Muslims, Reginald had vessels on the Mediterranean coast taken to pieces and transported on camels by Arabs across the desert to the Red Sea. There they were assembled and filled with adventurers who plundered the cities along the coast and amassed much booty. The raid was finally checked by the Muslims only when the Christians were within a day's march of Medina. The raiders were defeated after hard fighting, and only a few escaped. Some were taken to Mecca and beheaded; others were bound on camels and carried to Egypt to be killed. The Muslims felt outraged by the attempt to seize their holy places.

Saladin made a vow to kill Reginald if he ever got possession of him. But Reginald was to rule Karak for a few more years before his greed finally precipitated the fall of the kingdom of Jerusalem. Such adventurers as Reginald could nullify the peace policy followed by the Italian merchants and the leading nobles of the kingdom, and, by a single rash act, entail ruin for the Christians.

The Greek emperor had taken advantage of Reginald's humiliation to have himself acknowledged as lord of Antioch. In addition he had given his niece to King Baldwin III and had himself married a Frankish princess. After Baldwin III died, without children, his brother Amalric was also married to a Greek princess and attempted to work in harmony with the Greek emperor. For a few years the Greek emperor was recognized as the overlord of the kingdom of Jerusalem, and the king, when in the emperor's presence, sat humbly on a low seat by his side.

King Amalric, who was very able, hoped with the aid of the Greeks to capture Egypt. Ascalon, "the Bride of Syria," had been captured by Baldwin III in 1153, and now the time seemed propitious to extend the conquest. The Fatimite caliphate was much weakened by internal strife and seemed to be an easy prey, but the Franks were not the only ones who were attracted by the opportunity. To Nureddin the condition of Egypt was an occasion for an attempt to reconquer the land. One of the rival parties in Egypt sought aid from the Franks, the other from Nureddin.

For a number of years it was a question which would be heir to Egypt, the Crusaders or the Orthodox Muslims who held Mesopotamia and northern Syria. Neither party felt strong enough to attempt a decisive combat, and Amalric accepted large payments to withdraw his troops on condition that Nureddin's commander should also withdraw. A combined attack by the Greek emperor and the king of Jerusalem resulted in failure, and the long struggle only made it more easy for Nureddin's forces to get possession of Egypt and suppress the Fatimite caliphate. The alliance with the Greeks, instead of improving conditions between the Crusaders and the Greek Empire, really increased the hatred felt for the Greeks, because they had not carried on the expedition as earnestly as the Crusaders thought they ought to have done. The Greeks, as usual, had been hindered by the necessity of fighting against the Turks in Asia Minor, and in 1176 Emperor Manuel suffered a decisive defeat at Myriokephalon. After that the Greeks were no longer either a menace or an aid to the Frankish kings in Jerusalem.

CHAPTER VII

SALADIN AND THE LOSS OF THE KINGDOM

FROM all those engaged in the crusading wars romance has singled out Saladin as its own particular hero, with Richard the Lion-Hearted as a poor second. The choice was a natural one, for Saladin had the qualities which commended him to both Christian and Muslim. He did not have the broad tolerance in religion with which Lessing endowed him in *Nathan der Weise;* no Muslim leader could have had this tolerance; some of the Christian leaders in the Crusades came nearer to it through their acquaintance with the many religions they found in the Holy Land, and through their disillusionment with their own narrow inherited faith. Saladin did have the virtues of generosity and courtesy, with which Scott, following the example of medieval Christian writers, depicted him in *The Talisman.* He won the admiration of followers and enemies by his bravery. He never broke his word, a virtue which his opponents made use of, but did not imitate. Although he could be stern in his vengeance on occasion, he was usually merciful, and in this respect his character shines brilliantly against the barbaric background of the age. Many examples are recorded of his compassion for those in tribulation, especially Christian women and children. He was so open-handed and generous that his servants had to secrete funds lest he leave himself without necessary resources. When he died, the most powerful ruler in the Muslim world, he was almost penniless. Saladin, which means Honor of the Faith, was a name prophetic of his character and success.

He was a Kurd, born in 1137 or 1138 at Takrit, a fortress on the River Tigris, which his father held for the sultan. A few years before his birth Zangi, fleeing after a defeat, reached the Tigris on the bank opposite Takrit. His only chance of safety from his pursuers was in reception into the impregnable fortress. Saladin's father rescued the fugitive and thus laid the foundation for the future greatness of his family, for Zangi never forgot his debt of gratitude. The sultan, at Bagdad, was annoyed at Zangi's escape, and, when later Saladin's uncle killed a Muslim in a private quarrel, the sultan seized the excuse to order the family to give up Takrit and leave his dominions in disgrace. While they were in the midst of their preparations for departure Saladin was born. His birth at such a time was regarded as a bad omen.

His father sought the protection of Zangi at Mosul and found a ready welcome. The following year he was made commander of Ba'labakk, which Zangi had just captured. This was then an important and prosperous city, and Zangi's outpost against Damascus, only thirty-five miles away. Everyone is familiar with the magnificent ruins of the temples at Ba'labakk;

few people know that the temple ruins stand in the midst of a strong fortress, admirably adapted for defense in the days before cannon were invented; the walls with their subterranean passages are still well preserved and would be famous even if they did not contain the temple of Bacchus and the temple of the sun. There Saladin spent his early childhood.

When Zangi died the ruler of Damascus recovered Ba'labakk, but Saladin's father was given a fief near Damascus, and soon rose to be commander in chief of the army. When Nureddin secured Damascus in 1154 Saladin's father was made governor of the city, as he had prudently thrown in his lot with the son of his old patron. Nothing is known of Saladin's life during these years, although a Christian chronicler refers to a captivity which Saladin spent in Karak, the great fortress in the land of Moab. The Arab chroniclers record of him that he had "excellent qualities," and that he learned "to walk in the path of righteousness, to act virtuously, and to be zealous in fighting the infidels"—all commonplaces. Apparently there is nothing to tell until Saladin at the age of twenty-six took part in an expedition against Egypt, the land which later he ruled and loved better than any other. In the midst of one of his campaigns in Mesopotamia he wrote a poem, "Bear me a message to the Nile,— tell it that Euphrates can never quench my thirst."

Yet at first there was little hint of his future greatness or of his love for Egypt. He acquitted himself well on the first two expeditions to Egypt, but when his uncle was planning the third, which was destined to be the foundation of Saladin's fortunes, he was unwilling to go and was forced to do so only by the command of Nureddin. "'So I went,' said Saladin, recounting the scene in later years, 'I went like one driven to my death.' Thus were accomplished the words of the Koran: 'Perchance ye hate a thing although it is better for you, and perchance ye love a thing although it is worse for you: but God knoweth and ye know not.'" At thirty years of age Saladin was embarked on his life work. The remaining twenty-five years of his life were spent mainly in warfare. Only between the battles or in the intervals of truce could he find opportunity to engage in the theological discussions which he enjoyed.

The army sent by Nureddin was received by the Fatimite caliph of Egypt as an ally, and Saladin's uncle was soon made vizier and commander in chief of the Egyptian army. When he died, two months later, Saladin was appointed to succeed him. From this time on he "put aside the thought of pleasure and the love of ease, adopted a Spartan rule, and set it as an example to his troops. He devoted all his energies henceforth to one great object—to found a Muslim empire strong enough to drive the infidels out of the land. 'When God gave me the land of Egypt,' said he, 'I was sure that he meant Palestine for me also.'" "He had vowed himself to the Holy War." Many preliminary conquests were necessary, and many years were to intervene before he could address himself to this main task.

The next five years were spent in consolidating

his position as ruler of Egypt. At first he was in great difficulties; the other emirs in Nureddin's army envied him and were insubordinate. The Egyptian officials plotted his murder. A revolt broke out in the Sudan and lasted for years. Damietta was attacked by an army of Crusaders and Greeks. By his prudence and by the aid of his father and brothers whom he had summoned to Egypt, Saladin overcame all obstacles. When the caliph died in 1171 Saladin took possession of the palace at Cairo and all its treasures, but he would not live in the palace, and he kept none of the treasures; part he distributed to his followers; part he sent to his overlord, Nureddin. The latter looked on Saladin's advancement with displeasure as he realized that the Kurd was becoming a rival power. Saladin used all deference to him but was unwilling to meet him, believing that his power and life would both be at stake if he fell into Nureddin's hands. He never felt safe until he received the news of Nureddin's death.

That opened to him his opportunity. His power was firmly established in Egypt. In Syria Nureddin's successor was a young boy, and his followers took advantage of his weakness to throw off their allegiance and to seize his lands. In the kingdom of Jerusalem the king died the same year, leaving as his heir a boy of thirteen. To a less sagacious ruler than Saladin the time might have seemed ripe to make war upon the Christians. He had already engaged in skirmishes with them and had besieged, usually in vain, some of their fortresses. But Saladin knew that if the Holy War was to be successful it must be waged with all the forces of the Muslims united. Even Nureddin had been able to accomplish comparatively little without the support of the Egyptian troops. Saladin needed the aid of the Syrian and Mesopotamian Muslims before he could undertake the Holy War.

He spent the next two years in getting control over the Muslims in Syria. There his greatest obstacles were the rulers of Aleppo, but he was especially annoyed by the sect of the Assassins, who were probably incited against him by the Muslim ruler of Aleppo. Saladin narrowly escaped assassination by the followers of the dreaded "Old Man of the Mountains." After two years he was master of Muslim Syria. He had some indecisive battles with the Christians, but as yet he was not able to put forth all his strength against them, for the Muslim chiefs in Mesopotamia were still hostile and ready to attack him at any time when it was safe to do so. In 1180 he succeeded in negotiating a truce by which he was recognized as the chief Muslim ruler from the Euphrates to the Nile. He then returned to his beloved Egypt and remained there for the two years of the truce. He had also made a truce with the Christians. But Saladin was the only one who had sworn the truces who kept them. In spite of many provocations he refused to fight until the time of the truce with the other Muslims had expired. Then he left Egypt, which he was fated never to see again, and went north to conquer Mesopotamia. By 1183 he had succeeded, and when he wrote to the pope at Rome he used the title "King of all the Oriental Kings." The only lands left to recover were those in the hands of the Christians.

After the death of the chivalrous King Amalric (possibly the most intelligent of all the kings of Jerusalem), the kingdom had been weakened by internal dissensions. His son and successor, Baldwin IV, had been carefully educated by William, later archbishop of Tyre, the historian, and gave great promise of both ability and character. But as a child he was partially paralyzed, and when his father borrowed the services of eminent native physicians they diagnosed the malady as leprosy. The ill-starred king who reigned only ten years is known as Baldwin the Leper. For his guardian the barons at first chose Raymond, count of Tripolis. He was descended both from Count Raymond of Toulouse, who participated in the First Crusade, and from King Baldwin II. He was the ablest among the crusading leaders. In addition to his hereditary county of Tripolis, he had secured by his marriage with the heiress the strongly fortified Tiberias on the Lake of Galilee. He was a friend of Saladin; this friendship later made him distrusted by many in the kingdom and has raised a question among historians of the Crusades as to his good faith. But he had the full confidence of William of Tyre and of other Christians who had been born in the Holy Land.

Inasmuch as the kingdom, like the fiefs in the Holy Land, was hereditary even in the female line, the illness of the king made it essential to find a hus-

band for the king's elder sister Sibyl. The choice fell
on William of Montferrat, who was a relative of
both Philip Augustus of France and Frederick Barbarossa of Germany. But he lived less than a year
and died before the birth of his son Baldwin, who
was later to be king. Strangely enough, for three years
no new husband was found for the widow. Then the
king hastily married her to Guy of Lusignan, an ad-
venturer from France. This marriage was much condemned by the native nobles because Guy was
unpopular and considered stupid, but he was beautiful as a picture and had won the love of Sibyl. The
unsuitableness of the marriage and the indecent haste
with which Baldwin pushed it, celebrating the wedding, contrary to custom, in the midst of Lent, led
to a report that the king had determined on the marriage only to cover up the guilty love of his sister.
The more probable version of the marriage is that
the king gave his consent to it and was induced to
hasten the ceremony because of the imminent arrival of many of the barons in Jerusalem for the
Easter festivities. It was a foregone conclusion that
they would object to the princess' marrying a new-
comer from the West, and if the marriage had the
king's approval it would be better to confront the
barons with a *fait accompli* than to allow time for
their opposition to crystallize.

In 1183 Saladin made an invasion of the kingdom.
To meet the threatened peril the Christians raised
the largest force the kingdom had ever put into the
field. They were joined by some great nobles, pil-

grims from Europe, and the army moved against
Saladin. But King Baldwin was too ill to lead the
host,—too ill, even, to be carried in a litter to the
field of battle, as was his custom,—and he had entrusted the command of the army to Guy. The other
leaders refused to obey Guy, because, as they said,
he was a man "unknown and of little skill in military matters." But even William of Tyre implies
that Guy was not entirely to blame. The other barons
resisted aggressive action, it was said, in order that
Guy might not receive the credit of a victory. After
the armies had faced one another for a week of inac-
tion, Saladin withdrew, and the Christian army retired without striking a blow.

The dissatisfaction with Guy was so great that at a
council held in Jerusalem it was determined to crown
Baldwin, the king's nephew, son of Sibyl by her first
husband, and to entrust the regency to Raymond of
Tripolis for ten years. The boy was only six years
old. To quote Ernoul, a contemporary: "When the
matter was thus settled, the king bade crown the
child. So they led him to the Sepulchre and crowned
him. And because the child was small, they put him
into the arms of a knight to be carried into the Temple of the Lord, to the end that he might not appear
to be of less stature than the rest. This knight was a
stalwart man and tall." The king also proposed to
dissolve the marriage of Guy and his sister.

But the latter were safe in their city of Ascalon
and were not without friends. While most of the
nobles sided with Raymond, Guy and Sibyl had two

devoted adherents; Reginald of Chatillon, lord of Karak, was on their side, and also Gerard of Ridefort. The latter was a knight errant from England who had come to Syria. He had entered the service of Raymond of Tripolis and made himself so useful that he was promised the first wealthy heiress of whom Raymond had the disposal. Soon after, the lord of Botroun died, and his daughter was the coveted prize. Gerard expected to receive her and her fief. But a wealthy Italian merchant also coveted the prize and bought the heiress from Raymond. The girl is said to have been placed on the scale and balanced with her weight in gold, which the Italian paid for her. Gerard was very indignant, especially because a despised Italian merchant had been preferred to him. He left the count's service and, entering the Order of Templars, soon became grand master. His chief purpose in life was vengeance on Raymond.

Baldwin the Leper died before Easter of 1185, and the child king the following year. Unfortunately there is a gap in the amount and quality of historical evidence for the East between 1184 when William of Tyre ceased writing and 1190 when the Crusaders from the West reached the Holy Land. Ernoul, who continued the history of William of Tyre, was more inclined to accept rumor and gossip. Some account, however, of the events of 1186-87 can be pieced together from the various sources of the period. After the child's death, Gerard and Reginald of Chatillon saw their chance. They summoned Guy and Sibyl to come to Jerusalem; they closed the city gates and allowed no one to enter or leave. Their plan was to forestall Raymond and the native nobles by crowning Sibyl and Guy. They won over the patriarch of Jerusalem, who was said to be the lover of Sibyl's mother. The people were assembled in the Church of the Holy Sepulchre and two crowns were brought. Reginald proposed the choice of Sibyl as queen, and the pliant throng cheered for the daughter of Amalric, the mother of the late king, and the sister of the preceding one. After crowning her the patriarch said, "Lady, you are but a woman, wherefore it is fitting that you should have a man to support you in your rule. Take the crown before you and give it to him who can best help you to govern your realm." Sibyl then crowned Guy, saying: "My lord, receive this crown for I know not where I could bestow it better." Gerard of Ridefort is reported to have said: "This crown is well worth the marriage of Botroun."

Raymond and the native lords were very wroth and, rather than recognize Guy and Sibyl, chose as king, Humphrey, the step-son of Reginald and husband of Sibyl's younger sister. He was afraid to undertake the office and hastened to Jerusalem to seek Sibyl. She had heard nothing about the plan to make him king, but was angry with him and would not speak to him. "He stood before her," says the chronicler, "scratching his head like a shamefaced child," and muttering something about their wanting to make him king by force. When Sibyl understood what he was saying she quickly made him welcome.

After Humphrey had made his peace with Guy and

Sibyl, almost all the other nobles recognized them as sovereigns, because aside from Sibyl and Humphrey's wife there were no other legitimate heirs of Baldwin. Raymond of Tripolis remained obdurate. Gerard of Ridefort urged Guy to attack Raymond, and the king gathered a force to besiege him in Tiberias. But Raymond sought aid from Saladin, who sent troops, and the king did not dare to attack him. Raymond as regent had made a truce with Saladin which was very necessary to the Christians. New recruits were expected from the West, and Henry II of England had already sent large sums of money to the Holy Land for the expenses of the holy war. But all the Christians' hopes were shattered by an act of Reginald of Chatillon. During 1186 the caravans from Egypt and to Mecca had passed along the road under the walls of Karak, and Reginald had contented himself with levying tolls upon them. He had been absent from his fief much of the time, plotting for Guy's coronation or in attendance upon him. Toward the end of the year he was informed by his spies that an unusually large caravan was coming from Egypt. It was too much for Reginald's cupidity, and he again violated a truce by seizing all the treasures in the caravan and making the Muslims prisoners. It is reported that one of Saladin's sisters was travelling with the caravan under the escort of the merchants. "The taking of that caravan was the ruin of Jerusalem," says a Christian chronicler.

Saladin demanded satisfaction from King Guy, who attempted to make Reginald give up the booty. The latter replied that he was lord of his lands just as the king was of his, and that he had no truce with Saladin. He refused absolutely to return any of the prisoners or booty, and Guy was powerless to make him do so.

Saladin took a new oath that he would kill Reginald with his own hand and prepared for war. No attack could be attempted until the end of the rainy season. In the meantime Saladin summoned his forces from Egypt and the north coast of Africa, from Syria and Mesopotamia, determined upon a war which should make him master of all the Christian possessions. He would lead "the army of Paradise against the damned of Hell."

The danger to the Christians was imminent. All the resources of the kingdom were used to equip an army. Some of the money which Henry II had sent was taken to hire soldiers. Many pilgrims who came in the spring were pressed into the service. But as yet Raymond was not reconciled to Guy. His aid was absolutely necessary, and Guy sent ambassadors, the heads of the two military orders, the Hospital and the Temple, and others, to Tiberias to make peace with him.

In the meantime Saladin had sent a part of his army to the Lake of Tiberias under the command of one of his sons. This son asked permission from Raymond to cross the Jordan and make an expedition through his territory. The object of the excursion is not known. Raymond did not feel able to refuse, as Saladin's friendship was his best protection against

Guy. He gave permission, provided that the Muslims should return the same day before sunset and should do no damage to any town or house. This was agreed upon, and Raymond gave orders that no Christian should venture outside the walls during the day. It happened that the king's ambassadors to Raymond entered his territory that very day and, learning from Raymond of the Muslim expedition, determined to attack it. Gathering what knights they could, some 130, without waiting for the foot-soldiers whom they had summoned, they fell upon the returning Muslims.

The grand master of the Hospitallers and all the other Christian knights were killed except Gerard of Ridefort and three of his Templars. The Muslims, carrying the heads of the Christians on their spears, passed exultantly under the walls of Tiberias and recrossed the Jordan at sunset. They had kept their promise to Raymond and had done no injury to any town or house.

The death of the grand master of the Hospital and of so many Christian knights spread dismay throughout the land. The feeling against Raymond was very bitter. Under the circumstances he thought it well to make his peace with Guy. His help was essential and was welcomed. It was agreed that all the available forces should be assembled at the Springs of Saffuriyah, just north of Nazareth, to repel the Saracen invasion. The host assembled, containing about 1200 knights, thousands of foot-soldiers, and many natives armed in the Saracen fashion. The whole may

have numbered between twenty and thirty thousand
men. The position at Saffuriyah was a strong one and,
in particular, there was an abundant supply of water.
This was especially necessary as it was June and the
heat was great.

Saladin crossed the Jordan and besieged Tiberias,
which was under the command of Raymond's wife.
His purpose was to force the Christians to leave their
strong position and march to attack him. He captured and sacked the city of Tiberias, but the citadel
was still held by Raymond's wife. She sent an urgent
appeal for aid to the Christian army. A council of
war was held. Gerard of Ridefort, Reginald of Chatillon, and others urged an immediate march to relieve
the countess. Raymond opposed this plan, pointing
out that the country through which they must pass
was destitute of water, that the ground was rocky, dis-
advantageous for the Christian cavalry, that their
only chance of success was in maintaining their position until Saladin was forced to attack. He protested
that this was the only wise course to pursue, although
it was his own lands which Saladin was laying waste
and his own wife and children who were besieged in
the citadel. Gerard and Reginald insulted him repeatedly, arguing the cowardice of leaving the countess in peril. But Raymond's arguments were so
weighty that the council decided to follow his advice.
Late in the evening they separated, resolved to defend their position. But Gerard, knowing King Guy's
weakness and hatred of Raymond, followed him to
his tent and persuaded him to neglect the advice of

the council and to order an immediate advance. This the king did, and at daybreak the army set out to attack Saladin at Tiberias. The distance was about twenty miles.

All day long the heavily armed warriors marched through a parched land; the heat was intense on the shadeless glaring limestone roads; their water bottles were soon emptied. They were surrounded by light-armed Saracens who poured on them a hail of arrows. The rear guard of Templars was so hard pressed that they could not keep up with the main host. Seeing their peril, King Guy ordered a halt, and they camped for the night, although only about half of the distance to Tiberias had been covered and there was no water. The Saracens surrounded the camp so closely that one chronicler says not even a cat could have gotten out. The Muslims were jubilant. It was the night of Qadr, the most holy night, the night of predestination when Gabriel and the angels descend to earth; the night that is better than a thousand months; the night of power. All night long the Muslims raised their cry, "Allah is great, there is no God but Allah."

The following morning, the fourth of July, 1187, the Christians again straggled onward, crazed with thirst. Their distress was aggravated by the smoke and flames from the fires which the Saracens had set in the dry grass and which a high wind carried over to the Christian lines. The knights and foot-soldiers became separated. Guy ordered Raymond to charge the enemy, hoping to break their line. As Raymond

THE HORNS OF HATTIN

charged, according to one account, the Saracens opened their lines to let his men through; those with Raymond were the only ones to escape. Guy and some others took refuge on one of the Horns of Hattin, the site to which tradition assigns the Sermon on the Mount. The Horns are the remains of an ancient volcano and rise about two hundred feet above the level of the surrounding plain. The top was covered with boulders which made it impossible for the knights' horses to charge. The Lake of Galilee, or Tiberias, was in full sight to torture them in their thirst. The hot wind blew from the desert. The Christians fought bravely and desperately, but in vain. All except those who had been with Raymond and a few who became apostates were either killed or captured. A single Muslim soldier would be seen leading off thirty or more naked Christians, tied together with tent ropes.

Guy, Reginald, Gerard, and the other leaders were tied up and taken to Saladin's tent. First, all the Templars except the grand master, Gerard, were put to death. As King Guy was trembling and tortured with thirst, Saladin ordered brought to him rose water cooled with snow. Guy drank part and then handed the cup to Reginald, who emptied it. "But the Sultan," to quote the Muslim biographer, "turning toward the King, cried impetuously, 'You have not asked my permission to give a drink to that accursed one, the most criminal of the impious. I am not bound to spare his life. Do not give him another drink; I don't wish to have anything in common with this traitor. In giving him one drink you have not obtained my pardon for him and my protection does not extend to him.' He said that because of the rites of hospitality among the Mussulmans. It is one of the praiseworthy customs of the Arabs, one of their noble usages, that a captive has his life spared if he has eaten or drunk at the table of his captor, and it is to this generous custom that the Sultan made allusion."

While Saladin allowed the king and the others to be led away to refresh themselves, he left Reginald bound, lying in the vestibule of the tent. Later he summoned the king and the other chiefs. Then he heaped reproaches on Reginald for his crimes, enumerated his perfidies, saying, "Twice I have made a vow to God to kill you if I got hold of you, first when you tried to capture Mecca and Medina, second, when you treacherously seized the caravan." Then following the invariable custom, he commanded his prisoner to become a Muslim, and when Reginald refused he killed him. Guy was terrified, but Saladin comforted him saying, "Do not tremble,—a king does not kill a king." Reginald's head was carried to all the cities and castles in Egypt and Syria.

Then Saladin swept over the Holy Land. Only small garrisons had been left in the cities and castles. An anonymous letter writer tells what happened: "After this Saladin collected his army again and on Sunday came to *Saphora* [Saffuriyah] and took *Saphora* and Nazareth, and Mount Tabor, and on Monday came to *Acon* [Acre] which is also called *Acris;* and those in *Acon* surrendered. Likewise those

of *Caifas* [Haifa] and those of *Cesarea* [Caesarea]
and of *Jafa* [Joppa], and of *Naple* [Neapolis, Nabu-
lus], and of *Ram* [Ramlah], and of St. George, and of
Ybelinon [Ibelin], and of *Bellefort* [Belfort], and
of Mirabel, and of *Tyron* [Tyre], and of Gwaler, and
of *Gazer* [Gaza], and of *Audurum* [Darum], all surrendered." In three months he was master of most of
them. Jerusalem had to surrender on October second. The commander there was Balian of Ibelin, who
had escaped from Hattin, probably with Raymond.
(The latter died, it is said by western writers, of
shame shortly after the battle. Eastern writers give
the cause of death as pleurisy.) But Balian, knowing
Saladin's courtesy, sent to him asking for a safe conduct to go to Jerusalem, in order that he might take
his wife and children away. Saladin gave the safe
conduct on condition that Balian should remain only
one night in Jerusalem and should never fight against
him again. Balian took an oath that he would not.
But when he reached Jerusalem, the people urged
him to take command and the patriarch absolved
him from his oath. Yet Saladin showed no anger
against him and released him when he was again
captured. The sultan did not expect the Christians
to keep their oaths.

The city of Jerusalem had been defended with
great valor but at length was forced to treat of surrender. Saladin granted very merciful terms. The
well-to-do could ransom themselves; the poor were to
be ransomed for a lump sum—forty days were allowed
to collect the money. Then those who were not ran-

somed were to be slaves. "Never did Saladin show himself greater than during this memorable surrender." A Christian chronicler who was present says that Saladin's guards kept such order that no Christian suffered any ill-usage. Those who could, ransomed themselves. The remainder of King Henry II's treasure was used to ransom seven thousand of the poor. One of Saladin's emirs ransomed a thousand Armenians and sent them home. But the rich Christians took no thought for their poorer fellow-citizens and went away with all the treasure they could carry. The patriarch carried off all his own wealth, the treasures of the churches, and even the gold plate from the Holy Sepulchre. Saladin's officers remonstrated with him for letting the patriarch carry off so much treasure, but Saladin contemptuously let him do it. Thousands of the poor still remained unransomed. Then Saladin's brother begged the gift of a thousand and set them free. The patriarch and Balian also begged for some and were given another thousand to set free. Then Saladin said, "My brother has made his alms, and the patriarch and Balian have made theirs; now I would fain make mine." So he freed all the old people in the city. Ernoul, Balian's squire, the chronicler already quoted, says, "Such was the charity which Saladin did, of poor people without number." And he adds: "Then I shall tell you of the great courtesy which Saladin showed to the wives and daughters of knights, who had fled to Jerusalem when their lords were killed or made prisoners in battle. When these ladies were ransomed and had come

forth from Jerusalem, they assembled and went before Saladin crying mercy. When Saladin saw them
he asked who they were and what they sought. And
it was told him that they were the dames and damsels
of knights who had been taken or killed in battle.
Then he asked what they wished, and they answered
for God's sake have pity on them; for the husbands
of some were in prison, and of others were dead, and
they had lost their lands, and in the name of God
let him counsel and help them. When Saladin saw
them weeping, he had great compassion for them,
and wept himself for pity. And he bade the ladies
whose husbands were alive to tell him where they
were captives, and as soon as he could go to the
prisons he would set them free. (And all were released wherever they were found.) After that he commanded that to the dames and damsels whose lords
were dead there should be handsomely distributed
from his own treasure, to some more and others less,
according to their estate. And he gave them so much
that they gave praise to God and published abroad
the kindness and honour which Saladin had done to
them."

The contrast between this scene and the capture
of Jerusalem by the Crusaders in 1099 offers some
index of the difference in character and degree of
civilization between Saladin and the Christian leaders. It is not even necessary to go back to the First
Crusade for an example of the different standards.
Balian's squire tells us that the refugees from Jerusalem were refused admittance to Tripolis and were

robbed by their fellow-Christians of the property which Saladin had allowed them to carry away. Four years later Acre was captured by Richard the Lion-Hearted and Philip Augustus, and terms were granted to the Muslim inhabitants similar to those granted to the Christians at Jerusalem by Saladin. But when the ransom was not paid promptly Richard the Lion-Hearted ordered twenty-seven hundred of his hostages to be led out and slaughtered in cold blood before the eyes of the other Muslims—Richard was no Saladin. And his Christian chronicler added, "Nor was there any delay. The king's followers leapt forward eager to fulfill the commands, and thankful to the Divine Grace that permitted them to take such a vengeance."

Fortunately this example of Christian barbarity did not take place until after Saladin's conquests were over; otherwise he might have found it difficult to restrain his followers. At the surrender of the remaining positions held by the Christians he continued to show his accustomed clemency. At the siege of Ascalon Saladin promised Guy his freedom and that of the other leaders, if he would persuade the garrison to surrender. There was some delay on the part of the garrison, but they finally yielded. Whether Guy was at all influential in persuading them to capitulate is uncertain. At all events, Sibyl demanded that Saladin should fulfill his promise. Guy, Gerard, and the others were released and pledged their knightly honor that they would never again fight against Saladin. It is scarcely necessary to say that they did not keep their oath; as the Christian chronicler says, "The king was released by the sentence of the clergy from the enormity of this promise." The Saracens placed so little faith in an oath made by the Christians that on one occasion at least they would not accept an oath from the king unless it was sworn to by the Templars also. But in this case the grand master was equally guilty of perjury.

Saladin's conquest of the Holy Land was so nearly complete that Tyre was the only city that remained in the hands of the Christians. This Saladin began to besiege, but after a council of war raised the siege and dismissed most of his troops. They were weary of the long fighting and demanded a furlough, so that they might return to their homes and wives. Probably their unwillingness to continue the siege was the turning point in Saladin's victorious career. He had dreamed of driving all the Christians out of the Holy Land and then carrying the war into their country.

The kingdom of Jerusalem had been founded by Baldwin I in 1100; its power really ended with the capture of Jerusalem in 1187. For over a hundred years longer there was to be a nominal kingdom in the Holy Land. Jerusalem was to be recovered by the diplomacy of Frederick II and held for a period of fifteen years, from 1229 to 1244. The title of king of Jerusalem was to be used by one or more claimants continuously for centuries after the loss of the last Christian possessions in the Holy Land in 1291.

Except for Frederick II's Crusade the only serious attempt to recover the kingdom was the Third Crusade, in which Richard the Lion-Hearted, after the capture of Acre and after more than a year of fighting with alternate successes and reverses, was compelled to make a peace with Saladin by which the Christians retained the coast cities from Acre to Jaffa, which they had reconquered. Right of free passage was granted to both Muslim and Christian in the territory held by either party; and Christian pilgrims were allowed to visit the Holy Sepulchre at Jerusalem.

A year earlier Richard had suggested very different terms of peace. He proposed that Saladin's brother, Saphadin (Sayf al-Din), should marry his sister, the widowed queen of Sicily. Richard would give to his sister as a dowry Acre and the other cities which the Christians had taken. Saladin should give his brother the rest of Palestine, and the couple should reign at Jerusalem. The True Cross which the Saracens had captured should be restored and prisoners should be freed. The knights of the Temple and of the Hospital should receive suitable establishments. Richard admitted to Saphadin that the Christians blamed him for wishing to see his sister married to a Muslim and that his sister objected to the match. Richard suggested that Saphadin might become a Christian. These propositions do not seem to have been taken seriously by Saladin, but his brother continued to visit Richard, and "On Palm Sunday, 1192," the Christian chronicler tells us, "King Richard, amid much splendor, girded with the belt of knighthood the son of Saphadin, who had been sent to him for that purpose." In this, Saladin's nephew was following his uncle's example, for years before Saladin had been admitted to the honor of knighthood by one of the Christian lords of Palestine.

Richard and Saladin never met, although they frequently fought against each other and long negotiations were carried on by them. Richard finally had to leave the Holy Land without seeing Jerusalem. Saladin died a few months later, at the age of fifty-five. His physician wrote that this was the only time that he knew of when a sovereign was truly mourned for by his people. The reason for their grief may be seen from the instructions which Saladin, shortly before his death, gave to his favorite son—"My son, I commend thee to the Most High God, the fountain of all goodness. Do His will, for that way lieth peace. Abstain from the shedding of blood; trust not to that; for blood that is spilt never slumbers. Seek to win the hearts of thy people, and watch over their prosperity; for it is to secure their happiness that thou art appointed by God and by me. Try to gain the hearts of thy emirs and ministers and nobles. I have become great as I am because I have won men's hearts by gentleness and kindness." The resemblance of this advice to the instructions which Saint Louis of France left, three-quarters of a century later, for his son, is very striking. In many respects Saint Louis and Saladin had much in common. Both were ascetic; Saladin may have shortened his life by his zeal in fasting in order to make up for the periods of fasting he had been compelled to neglect during his wars against the Christians. Both kings had the gift of tears, so highly prized by the Christians of the Middle Ages. Saladin would listen to the reading of the Koran until his ecstasy was so great that the tears would roll down his cheeks. The words of his biographers in relating this might well have been borrowed by a Christian chronicler to describe the devotion of his hero, e.g., Suger, abbot of S. Denis and regent of France, who during the office of the Mass "inundated the pavement with his tears."

Richard the Lion-Hearted prided himself upon being the best knight in Christendom. Saladin the Muslim surpassed him in some of the knightly virtues. His Christian opponents praised him especially for his courtesy. One of them, in recounting the story of Saladin's first siege of Karak, says that Reginald of Chatillon and his wife were celebrating the marriage of her son Humphrey with the younger daughter of King Amalric at the very time when Saladin invested the castle. Reginald's wife sent to Saladin some of the viands from the wedding banquet with a greeting and a reminder of how many times Saladin had carried her about in his arms when he was a captive at Karak and she was a little girl. Saladin was much pleased and thanked her for the gift. Then he asked in which part of the castle the newly wedded pair resided and forbade any attack upon that side of the castle. At the siege of Jaffa, Ernoul says that Saladin heard that Richard was in the town and had no horse on which to fight; consequently Saladin sent Richard a splendid charger. During the siege of Acre

a Christian woman went to the Muslim camp begging
for her baby, who had been carried off by the Saracens. The pickets let her pass and conducted her to
Saladin, "for," they said, "he is very merciful."
"Saladin was touched by her anguish; the tears stood
in his eyes, and he had the camp searched" till the
little girl was found. She was restored to her mother
and both were escorted back to the enemy's camp.
The act was characteristic of Saladin.

CHAPTER VIII

IMPORTANCE OF THE KINGDOM OF THE CRUSADERS

"EACH age studies its history anew, and with interest determined by the spirit of the time." This dictum is illustrated by the varying opinions which have been held about the importance of the Crusades.

The point of view of the early Crusaders is well represented by the words of Robert the Monk, who wrote in the prologue to his history of the First Crusade: "If we except the salutary mystery of the crucifixion, what has happened since the creation of the world that is more marvellous than this which has been done in modern times, on this expedition of our men to Jerusalem? The more studiously anyone directs his attention to this subject, the more fully will the convolutions of his brain expand and the greater will be his stupefaction. For this was not the work of man but the work of God." Many contemporaries would have subscribed to the Monk's statement. Fulcher of Chartres, who went on the First Crusade, has given a vivid account of the scene when the Crusaders left their homes, their families, and all that was dear to them. He sums up his own and their feelings with the text: "This is the Lord's doings and it is marvellous in our eyes."

Interest in Crusades continued long after the lands which the early Crusaders had won were all lost. Christopher Columbus—to mention only one instance —was interested not only in discovering the way to the Indies, but also in helping the cause of the Crusades. The two objects were closely bound together in his thoughts. In his journal, under the date of December 26, 1492 (i.e., while he was on his first voyage) he stated that he wished all the profit of his undertaking to be spent in the conquest of Jerusalem, and that he believed that the Spanish sovereigns had promised to do this. When writing his will, he was still intent upon furthering the cause of the Crusades, and he directed the creation of a trust fund which should be used for a Crusade. It was this feeling which influenced Tasso in the last third of the sixteenth century when he was writing his *Jerusalem Delivered*. Indeed, another Crusade was then being planned, and Tasso may have been inspired by the desire to arouse his contemporaries to action.

Though active efforts ceased, men continued to read and write about the Crusades. Without pausing to consider all the periods, we may turn to Thomas Fuller, who in his *Holy War*, written in the seventeenth century, conceived of the Crusades as a defensive war. "Thus after a hundred ninety and four years ended the Holy War; for continuance the longest, for money spent the costliest, for bloodshed the cruelest, for pretences the most pious, for the true intent the most politic the world ever saw. And at this day, the Turks, to spare the Christians their pains of coming so long a journey to Palestine, have done them the unwelcome courtesy to come more than half the way to give them a meeting."

In the following century when the Turks were no longer a menace, Voltaire poured forth his scorn upon the movement: "Then for the first time appeared this epidemic fury, in order that there might be no possible scourge which had not afflicted the human race." "Thus, the only fruit of the Christians in their barbarous Crusades was the extermination of other Christians." Gibbon held practically the same opinion but noted that "Those who remained at home, with sense and money, were enriched by the epidemical disease."

This superficial point of view did not long prevail. In 1806 the National Institute of France offered a prize for the best essay on the influence of the Crusades. This occasioned the writing of several books, two of which are excellent. About the same time Wilken in Germany and Michaud in France began their long histories of the Crusades. The spirit of romanticism seized upon this crusading period as peculiarly its own.

In the nineteenth century the idea of a defensive war was again popular. Sybel gave it currency: "We cannot understand the importance of the Crusades if we look upon them as a mere sequel and extension of the pilgrimages to Jerusalem. Such a complete change in the history of the world does not arise out of such insignificant causes. The Crusades must be regarded as one great portion of the struggle between the two great religions of the world, Christianity and Mohammedanism." Some of the chief authorities on the history of the Crusades, Riant, Hagenmeyer, Röhricht, Kugler, held this opinion. But the last, Kugler, following in the footsteps of Heeren, considered the Crusades especially important for another reason: "Among those who have critically studied the history of the middle ages it is a recognized fact that the Crusades were to a great extent the result of economic causes and that they must be studied as a part of the general history of colonization."

Ernest Barker sums up ably the present ideas: "The Crusades may be regarded partly as the *decumanus fluctus* in the surge of religious revival, which had begun in western Europe during the tenth century and had mounted high during the twelfth century; partly as a chapter, and most important chapter, in the history of the interaction of East and West.... They are again the 'foreign policy' of the papacy, directing the faithful subjects to the great war of Christianity against the infidels."

In considering the importance of the Crusades, "the interaction of East and West" should be stressed. As Jenks well said: "Mixture or at least contact of races is essential to progress." During the ninety years which ended with the capture of Jerusalem by Saladin, there had been many contacts and much mixture between the different peoples present in Syria and Palestine. The contacts and mixture were to continue for another hundred years. Moreover, on their way to the Holy Land, the different peoples of western Europe mixed together, imbibed impressions and ideas from one another, and also were influenced by the Greeks and Armenians through whose territories they went and whom they in turn influenced.

It is important that the chief scene of the contact was in Syria and Palestine. For these lands were much richer in natural products than the west of Europe and, in addition, had for many centuries been the entrepôt for wares which were luxuries, or unknown, in the West. When the Crusaders entered these lands, they found a much higher civilization than any to which they were accustomed. Antioch, Tripolis, and other cities were centers of industry and learning. Old traditions of workmanship had been preserved, as in glass making, dyeing, and manufacture of steel. Much of the old Greek knowledge of science, and especially of medicine, had been handed down from generation to generation, and other learning and arts with which the Arabs had come into contact in their conquests had been brought thither to enrich its culture. This learning was nurtured by the patronage of enlightened rulers like Nureddin and Saladin.

The Frankish conquerors soon began to imbibe some of the ideas they found in the East, as has been shown in Chapter V. Because of the needs of intercourse a *lingua franca* developed; this was a mixture of various languages and was commonly used by the people who resorted to the Greek and Syrian ports. It should be noted also that the Franks em-

ployed Arabic in their custom-houses in order to
facilitate trade with the interior. Naturally, few
scholars participated in the Crusades, and comparatively little of the Arabic learning seems to have been
introduced into the West through the Crusaders'
kingdom. But there were some exceptions. Bohadin
says that Reginald of Sidon was well versed in oriental sciences and literature and that he kept in his
service an Arab doctor whose duty it was to read and
explain to him the writings of oriental scholars.
When he visited Saladin all the Muslim doctors were
amazed at his prodigious learning in history and
literature. His son Balian is said to have been a very
learned man. William of Tyre says that Geoffrey,
abbot of the Temple of Our Lord, was one of the
most distinguished Hellenists of his age, and William
himself wrote an oriental history from the Arabic
sources. Other names might be mentioned, and possibly further research may add materially to our
knowledge of this subject. An excellent example of
the transmission of Arabic lore in the field of medicine is found in the fact that merchants from Montpellier, in France, brought home some Arabic physicians who taught medicine. In spite of the opposition
of the Christian doctors, the lord of the city gave
them the full privilege of teaching. Montpellier became the chief medical school north of the Alps and
was surpassed only by Salerno, which was itself a
center of Saracen teaching.

Almost every part of Europe was exposed in some
degree to the influence of the Crusader Kingdom in

the East. The number that went on the Crusades from the West was very large. Contemporaries were amazed at the wide extent of the movement: "Thus one saw an infinite multitude, speaking different languages and coming from divers countries." "There was no nation so remote, no people so retired as not to contribute its portion." The army of the First Crusade was said by Anna Comnena to outnumber the stars of the heaven or the sands of the shore—a statement of interest only in showing that their number was very large. Five years later an army of almost equal size went on the ill-fated expedition of 1101. Other armies numbering tens of thousands went on the Second, Third, and Fourth Crusades. Seignobos does not hesitate to write that there were millions who went on the Crusades. If he intends to include all who took the Cross and actually started at one time or another, his statement is probably true.

They went mainly from France, Germany, and Italy, but every country in Europe contributed a larger or smaller number. In this connection the monographs dealing with the Crusaders who were natives of various places are very instructive. There were relatively few pilgrims from the Scandinavian countries, yet Count Riant succeeded in gathering together a long list of names of Scandinavian leaders who participated in the Holy War. Others have compiled special lists for Norway, Denmark, England, Belgium, Holland, France, Switzerland, Germany, Spain, Portugal, and Italy. Local historians have care-

rully collected the records of those who went out
from Flanders, Normandy, Auvergne, Champagne,
Anjou, Picardy, Burgundy, Maine, Brunswick, Frisia,
Saxony, Bavaria, Piedmont, Lombardy, Pisa, Venice,
Piacenza, Naples, and many other localities. Moreover, these studies preserve the names only of those
who were conspicuous by their position or deeds; the
rank and file of the armies are never mentioned. The
numbers of unarmed pilgrims who filled the pilgrim
fleets for the Easter and Christmas arrival while the
Holy Land was held by the Crusaders were probably
even greater than the number of Crusaders. Surely
almost every corner of Europe had an opportunity
to learn something about the East from returned
Crusaders, from friends or relatives in the Holy Land,
or at least from returning pilgrims travelling through
their locality.

Constant communications were maintained with
the West. The Crusaders in the East needed men and
supplies, especially horses and lumber. On the other
hand, the men who returned from the Holy Land
had become acquainted with the new foods, spices,
sugar, muslin, silk, cotton, damask, samite, camel's
hair fabrics, and other luxuries of the East and were
eager to get them. From them the knowledge and
desire spread to others. The Italian cities found it
necessary to create a market for the booty which their
fleets had obtained in the East; for example, the
Genoese had to dispose of the thousands of pounds
of pepper which they had secured at Caesarea in
1101. The taste for the oriental luxuries spread

rapidly and the demand for them increased. The cost decreased because to transport the horses and lumber to the Holy Land required large vessels, and for the return voyage a cargo was needed. Most of the eastern luxuries represented a large value for little bulk, and the cost for freight was very little compared with the value of the articles. Venice, Genoa, Pisa, and Marseilles rapidly built up a lucrative trade, carrying supplies to the Crusaders and bringing back a cargo of eastern luxuries. The art of navigation improved and a rude compass came into use. It was soon possible and feasible to make journeys all the year around, and communication might be constant throughout the year.

Before the Crusades trade had been carried on mainly by barter; even the receipts of the kings of England from their sheriffs had been mainly in kind. To finance the expenses of a Crusade money was needed. The gold and silver which had been hoarded or used in ornaments had to be brought into circulation. To carry on the new trade a money economy was necessary. Money circulated more rapidly as the demand for it increased. When collections were made for a Crusade much of the money received was in copper which had to be changed with silver. The minters were busy in coining it. In transporting money to the Holy Land there were frequent losses, especially in the First Crusade. To meet the new needs a system of banking grew up, and the Templars became the most important agents. The chief banking center in the West was at Paris. There they received money on deposit which was to be used in the Holy Land, as for instance, from Henry II of England. To obviate the necessity of transporting the actual coins, they made use of what would now be termed letters of credit or bills of exchange. The accounts of their house at Paris for a period of nine months are still extant.

The higher standard of living, due to the desire for new foods, finer clothing, and larger castles, caused a great increase in the cost of living, and this resulted in a shifting of wealth and a change in the relative importance of the social classes. The nobles, whose incomes were relatively fixed, being derived mainly from customary payments, were the ones who felt the new needs most strongly. They wanted the spices and sugar, the fine clothes and armor. Silk dresses, camel's hair shawls, brocades, and oriental rugs became objects of desire. The emperors of Constantinople often gave rich costumes to the western leaders whose aid or neutrality they needed. These were highly appreciated and set the fashion for others. Cultivation of silk-worms and the manufacture of silk became more common in the West. At Paris they began to make imitations of oriental rugs, or Saracen carpets, as they were called. New tastes arose in food as well as in dress. Sugar had been used almost exclusively as a medicine. Its growth in all southern Europe spread rapidly and the use of sugar became general. Spices which were rare and costly after the immigrations in the fifth and sixth centuries now became common.[1] And these luxuries gradually, we must remember, became necessities. One indication of the relative cost of these new luxuries may be obtained from the price of the material for a lady's dress; if she had bought livestock instead, she could have obtained five horses, five pigs, and twenty geese.

The nobles also began to build larger and finer castles. Crusaders returning from the East spread throughout the West the knowledge of improvement in the art of war and the skill they had acquired in the construction of war machines. From the Byzantines they borrowed the use of Greek fire and finally its composition. From the Saracens they borrowed the cross-bow and the method of constructing a portcullis. The latter in Italian is still called the saracinesca. Changes in the form and construction of body armor were necessitated by conditions in the Holy Land. The chain armor of the eleventh century was sufficient defense against an ordinary arrow, but not protection against a quarrel, the shaft shot by a crossbow. Contact with these new missile weapons, and their use in West as well as East, caused the use of heavier—and more expensive—armor.

[1] It is interesting in this connection, to see how little was known about the origin and growth of these spices even in the thirteenth century. Joinville, the friend of St. Louis, says that "before the Nile enters Egypt the people spread their nets in the river at dusk. On the following morning they find in these nets the commodities which they sell by weight and which are brought to this country; namely, ginger, rhubarb, aloes wood, and cinnamon. And it is said that these things come from the terrestrial paradise; the wind blows down the trees which are in paradise just as in the forests of this country the wind blows down the dead wood. The dead wood which falls into the river is sold to us by the merchants in this country."

One of the virtues of the noble class was extravagance. Parents warned their sons against being niggardly and urged them always to give freely. The jongleurs praised only those who were freehanded. The result was that many of the nobles fell into debt. In the Pipe Roll of 1181-1182, we find a list of three hundred knights, poor debtors, from whom the king was unable to collect his dues. The lesser nobility were losing in importance and frequently had to sell their holdings. In one of the lays of a slightly later date the author states: "Once upon a time, more than a hundred years ago, there lived a rich villein whose name I cannot now tell, who owned meadows and woods and waters, and all things which go to the making of a rich man.... This sweet fief was builded by a certain knight, whose heir sold it to a villein; for thus pass baronies from hand to hand, and town and manor change their master, always falling from bad to worse."

The Jews were the chief money-lenders, and the rates of interest were excessively high. When the security was good, the Jews in England in the twelfth century charged two pence on the pound each week, compounded once in six weeks; this works out about fifty-two per cent a year. When the security was not so good the rate increased to three or four pence a week, and so consequently to about eighty per cent or one hundred twenty per cent a year. Impecunious and thriftless nobles could seldom free themselves from debt, and a feeling of resentment against the usurers grew. The Jews were long protected by the monarchs, who found them very useful, but a subtle propaganda gradually had its effect, resulting in persecutions and final expulsion from some of the countries. There were persecutions before the Crusades, and the worst treatment did not take effect until after the period of this volume, and not until there were Christian money-lenders to take the Jews' place.

The Christian merchants profited greatly by the increased economic activity. Benjamin of Tudela says, "We here, [in Palestine] met with Christian and Mohammedan merchants from all parts: from Algarve [Portugal]; Lombardy, the Roman Empire, Egypt, Palestine, Greece, France, Spain, and England. People of all tongues met here, chiefly in consequence of the traffic of the Genoese and Pisans." While the citizens in Northern Italy made the most rapid advances, those in the French cities, in Flanders, along the Rhine and the Danube, on the Baltic, and elsewhere, shared in the advance and were able to buy freedom from some of the servile restrictions and disabilities. "The Crusading movement and the consequent need for money amongst the ruling classes coincided with the growing wealth of the boroughs and the growing importance of the burgess class. It was a vital moment, and the communes took advantage of it. The result was a universal spread of communal associations." In France this movement had started before the First Crusade, but the twelfth century was a great period of growth. In order to secure money for the expenses of a Crusade or to meet the increased cost of living, caused by the new luxuries which were rapidly becoming quasi-necessities to the nobility, the ruling classes sold to the burgesses privileges and charters. Impoverished nobles had to sell their estates, as we have seen in the quotation from *The Lay of the Little Bird.* "Other tales, such as The Divided Horsecloth, tell of intermarriages between the nobility and the merchant class. St. Louis' well-known advice to his son testifies to the importance to which the citizens had attained."

Of course, not all this advance of the merchants was due to the Crusades; it had begun earlier and there were many other causes for it. But it is well to remember that "trade, as an independent occupation, grew up first in the service of luxury," and during the twelfth century it was the demand for the new luxuries from the Orient which so greatly stimulated the trade and enriched the merchants.

The trade was not confined to oriental goods. Manufactures increased in the West; e.g., the cloth of Arras became famous. In Paris in the thirteenth century there was a domestic production of "tapis saracenas." Genoa exported to the Orient great quantities of cloth which she did not herself manufacture but for which she was one of the great entrepôts.

One of the features of the age which best illustrates the rapid growth of international trade is the great increase in the number of fairs during the twelfth century. At these fairs in Champagne or at the Lendit in Paris, merchants gathered from all parts of Europe, and the people flocked thither not only to buy, but to enjoy the shows of acrobats and the varied activities of the fair. The many fairs in the different countries and the protection which they enjoyed caused an increase in the amount of travel and inter-communication of people.

This intercommunication caused a rapid spread of heresy, which followed along the routes of trade. One of the most widespread forms of heresy, the Manichean, was of eastern origin. To counteract this heresy, preaching and teaching by the orthodox was especially needed, as Bernard of Clairvaux pro-claimed. And the Crusades had led to a wider preva-lence and a new form of preaching, of which Peter the Hermit and Fulk of Neuilly were the most promi-nent examples. Their success in leading sinners to repentance called attention to the need of popular preaching and led to the widespread use of exempla, or sermon stories.

This was the golden age of story-telling. On the pilgrimages the men and women would eagerly listen to anyone who had something new to tell. In the castles and monasteries after dinner, in the market-place or in the narrow streets where the gildsmen worked, the story teller found an audience. And he had a much larger repertoire on which to draw, be-cause of the events of the Crusades. There were the songs which extolled the deeds of Peter the Hermit and Tafur, king of the Beggars, on the First Crusade. As time went on, there were many accounts of the unexpected return of Crusaders long believed dead and of knights who had been rescued from captivity by the love of Saracen princesses. Then, too, the mixture of so many peoples from different lands had caused the stories peculiar to one locality to become the common stock in trade of the participants. Many tales of oriental origin became common in the West. Throughout the literature of the twelfth and thirteenth centuries are many references to the products of the East: to the red gold of Araby; to the rich stuffs of the Orient, the silk, damask, samite; to the spices which were so highly prized.

History became more popular. Men and women were eager to know of the deeds of their kinsmen and neighbors. The scope of history was broadened to include the past of the enemies with whom the Crusaders contended. The songs were sung in the vernacular, and, a little later than the period we are treating, history, too, began to be written in the language of the people, to satisfy their demand for information. This can be traced most clearly in France, the land which was most concerned with the Crusades.

Men, too, were eager to know of the lands which were the scenes of the exploits and the home of the events of the Bible and of the new products which were the objects of such demand and the source of the increased wealth. The Crusades and the increased trade caused an enormous increase in the geographical knowledge of western Europe. Wright says,[2] possibly with some exaggeration, "it is safe to infer that practically every town and village of France, Eng-

[2] Wright, J. K., *Geographical Lore of the Time of the Crusades.* New York, 1925. Especially pp. 292ff.

land, Germany, and Italy held someone who had visited the East and was not unready to tell about what he had seen there and on his way out and back." "Through the reports brought back to Europe by returning soldiers, adventurers and merchants, Syria and Palestine became more richly and accurately known in the West than most parts of Europe itself." The itineraries and accounts of travel to the Holy Land which had begun centuries before the Crusades became more numerous and more detailed during the period of the Latin Kingdom. Much of the contents are mere enumerations of distances from place to place or of the holy sites to be visited, but there are also precious indications of the occupations of the people, as in Benjamin of Tudela, of the state of feeling among the Franks and natives, as in the passages already quoted from Ibn Jubayr, and of many other facts which make the history and conditions more vivid to us, as they did to contemporaries. Sometimes this knowledge took the form of legend rather than of accurate fact. Joinville, for instance, gives this hearsay account of the headwaters of the Nile. "They say that the Sultan of Babylon [Egypt] had attempted many times to find out where the river came from, and that he had sent people to find out.... They carried a kind of bread which they call biscuit, because it had been cooked twice [bis]; and they lived on this bread until they returned to the sultan. They reported that they had gone up the river and had come to a great perpendicular cliff which no one could climb. From this cliff the river fell; and it seemed to them

that there was a great abundance of trees on the top
of the mountain. And they said that they had found
marvellous wild animals of different forms, lions, ser-
pents, elephants, who had come to look at them from
above the bank of the river, while they were going
up stream." This description suggests the interest
which the men of the West felt in these eastern lands
which were to them the home of so many marvels.
All of the accounts of the expeditions are full of bits
of geographical knowledge, and the people of the
West were eager scholars.

The increased knowledge among the Franks of
medicine and of the other arts in which the Orientals
excelled has already been mentioned, and its effects
in producing an admiration for the followers of the
Prophet. This led to a desire in the West to know
something of their history and religion. The Abbot
Guibert, in his history of the First Crusade, gives a
curiously mixed account of Mohammed and his religion. Peter the Venerable, abbot of Cluny, was not
satisfied and had the Koran translated so that he
might know its contents. This change in attitude towards the Muslims is perhaps best exemplified by the
attempts to convert them—by persuasion rather than
by the Crusader's sword. The missionary journey of
Saint Francis of Assisi to infidel lands is well known.
A plan was formed to have oriental languages taught
at the University of Paris so that missionaries might
be trained in the use of the necessary tongues. Saint
Louis of France is said to have directed the Crusade
of 1270 to Tunis from the mistaken belief that the

ruler of that country was ready to receive baptism. Oliver the Scholastic wrote, in 1221, a letter to "the King of Babylon" urging him to accept Christian teaching, and another to the Doctors in Egypt, that is the learned Mussulmans. Jacques de Vitry also attempted to convert the Muslims. He says in one of his letters: "As I was not able to preach in the land of the Saracens, I showed the errors of their religion and the truth of ours by letters which I sent to them, written in the Saracen tongue." He was evidently acquainted with the work of Peter the Venerable, who also had wished to convert the Muslims. In the second half of the thirteenth century such authors as William of Tripoli, Humbert of Romans, Burchard of Mount Zion and Ricoldus show that not only was knowledge concerning the Saracens increasing in volume and in accuracy, but also that among some of the educated class the desire to convert the Muslims was still strong. The fame of Saladin and of the "Old Man of the Mountains" spread throughout the West and one became a hero and the other an object of wonder. The legends, already cited, which gave to Thomas Becket a Saracen mother, which made Nureddin the son of the Countess Ida of Austria who disappeared in the ill-fated Crusade of 1101, or the story of Beyond the Seas which recounted Saladin's descent from a daughter of the bluest blood of France, illustrate this admiration in the West for the Saracens.

This reference to the women of the other race as mothers of the great heroes suggests an interesting question. How far, if at all, was the new position which the lady, and especially the Virgin, came to hold in these ages a result of the Crusades? The question is a baffling one, and it would certainly be rash to attribute the chivalric veneration for the lady to any single cause. Yet I think it is possible that success by the noble chatelaines in management of the fiefs during the absence of their lords in the Holy Land may have contributed to the new position which women held. We need further study of the reasons for the rather sudden emergence of the lady of chivalry and of her greatly increased importance in the twelfth century.

The influence of the contact with the Muslims upon western life is doubtless the most important and most direct result of the Crusades. Even here, however, we must bear in mind the fact, of which we have already reminded ourselves, that there were other channels through which this Muslim influence might come. With that reservation, we may cite the use of sugar, of the drum and trumpet, the employment of the cross-bow as evidence of Latin contact with Muslim civilization. Very many of our common plants have been brought from the Orient, but only a few are definitely known to have been brought during the period of the Crusades; among these may be noted the Ascalonian garlic, watermelons, and a few others, including, probably, sesame and the apricot. A number of definite acquisitions of a miscellaneous character may be ascribed to the contact between the Franks and the natives during the Crusades. The art of heraldry grew up in Syria, and many of its terms betray their oriental origin. Family names also became common, because of the necessity of distinguishing one from another. Certain customs, such as the use of windmills and the wearing of beards, were introduced.

The Saracens do not seem to have borrowed much from the Frankish customs. Naturally, they did not care to imitate a civilization which they felt was inferior to their own. Very different was the attitude of the Armenians. While the Westerners were drawing freely from the culture of the Greeks and Saracens, they were in turn exercising a remarkable influence on the less advanced civilization of the Armenians in Cilicia. The latter, since they had left their former home, had gradually built up a strong state. When the first army of Crusaders appeared, the Armenians welcomed them eagerly and aided them in their battles. Their feelings are well expressed by Matthew of Edessa, who wrote that "the Franks came to break the chains of the Christians, to free the holy city of Jerusalem from the yoke of the infidel and to wrest from the hands of the Mussulmans the consecrated tomb which received a God."

During the following century there were among the Armenians two parties, bitterly antagonistic; one wished to retain the old customs, the other to introduce Frankish usages. The latter carried the day, possibly because the western customs were better adapted to the less advanced civilization. The movement was hastened by the frequent intermarriages between the crusading chiefs and the Armenian princesses. The

changes in ecclesiastical usages had become so pro-
nounced by the close of the twelfth century that the
conservative party got the ear of King Leo, who wrote
to Nerses of Lambron, bishop of Tarsus, command-
ing him to return to "the traditions of our fathers."
The bishop replied that the king ought to practice
what he preached and discard all Frankish usages.
The letter which the bishop wrote is most instructive.
It reads, in part, "But if it is difficult for your Majesty to abandon the excellent and refined usages of
the Latins, that is, the Franks, and go back to the
crude manners of the ancient Armenians; if you no
longer plait your hair, nor let your beard grow, and
if you have ceased now to wear loose, flowing garments, it would be still more difficult for us to do
away with, and despise the perfected institutions,
which we borrowed from the Franks, for the glory of
the Holy Church. . . . Because we found the Armenian
church without sacerdotal garments, we borrowed
them from the Latins and with their assistance we
have done away with the old usage. We saw that our
ecclesiastics united the third, sixth, and ninth hours
of common prayer. Relying on the example of the
Latins, we now celebrate each office at its proper hour,
and we praise God seven times a day. We found that
the ceremony of the peace was neglected in our convents; we re-established it. . . . We saw that they
[Franks] have regular charitable institutions for the
support of the poor. Eager to imitate this laudable
institution and as a tribute to your kindness, we are,
at the Church of Tarsus every Friday and Wednesday,

dividing bread and beans among two or three hundred poor people." It is very seldom that any such detailed statement of the influence of one people upon the customs of another has been set forth by a contemporary.

King Leo introduced a feudal system into his new kingdom and borrowed freely from the customs of Antioch. In the following century Sempad, Constable of Armenia, translated the Assizes of Antioch because, as he said, "our people and our court ordinarily use these assizes." By ignorance or carelessness, errors had crept in, and Sempad got an authentic copy, made a translation, and had it compared with the original. "Curiously enough, at the present day, our main source of information for the laws of the principality of Antioch is this copy in the Armenian language, made by Sempad, which was discovered by chance and published in 1876. It would be evident, without Sempad's statement, that these laws contain the usages of the Franks because they are often identical with those embodied in the Assizes of Jerusalem. The regulations on such subjects as marriage and inheritance were taken over by the Armenians in their entirety from the Norman customs of Antioch."

The other race whose contacts with the Franks in the East were important in the development of western civilization, the Greeks, contributed to rather than drew from Latin culture. They were, of all the eastern peoples, the most closely related to the westerners in culture and in religion. This community of background and the fact that they faced a common enemy predisposed the Latins at least, and probably the Greeks as well, to that friendship between peoples which favors mutual cultural borrowings.

The Greek emperor had appealed to the West for help against the Muslims and therefore may be assumed to have been favorably disposed toward the crusading armies. On the other hand, we must remember that previous friction with the Normans in southern Italy would have fostered a suspicious attitude towards some contingents at least in the crusading forces. To judge by the pages of Anna Comnena —which may reflect later events rather than a strictly contemporary viewpoint—the misunderstandings and indiscretions of the First Crusade added to these suspicious reservations on the part of the emperor rather than increased his friendliness for the Latins.

The Westerners more than shared this distrust. The misunderstandings and actual clashes in arms during the First Crusade left a heritage of distrust in the West. Raymond the Chaplain expresses the feeling of many of the Crusaders when he says that "as long as they live, the people will curse him and proclaim him [Emperor Alexius] a traitor" and, he continues, "we recognized then that the Emperor had betrayed Peter the Hermit." Alexius was blamed also for the failure of the Crusade of 1101. Bohemond, whose differences with Alexius were real enough though not one-sided, found little difficulty in raising a considerable army in the West for an attack .upon Alexius in 1107. Though the attack failed, the attitude of distrust and even hostility continued in the West, kept alive by repeated irritating incidents as pilgrims and Crusaders proceeded through Constantinople and across Asia Minor as long as the Latins held the Holy Land. The disasters which befell the armies of the Second Crusade in Asia Minor were, like the earlier disasters in the same region, blamed upon the Greek emperor.

The efforts of Emperor Manuel and his court to cultivate more friendly relations did little to abate this feeling. He genuinely admired Frankish customs and actually sought the honor of knighthood of the feudal West. Constantinople thronged with western merchants as well as pilgrims and Crusaders who enjoyed his favor. This friendly attitude reached its climax in the two weddings at Constantinople in the early months of 1180, witnessed by William of Tyre, in which the emperor's son married the daughter of the king of France and his daughter was married to Boniface of Montferrat, of the noble north Italian house. These efforts at friendship, however genuine and sincere on his part, were largely personal and scarcely outlasted his own lifetime. The fundamental rivalries of the two races were still existent, and the hatred the Franks originally felt only for the Muslims was continually and gradually being transferred to the Greeks who were commercial rivals of the Venetians, political enemies of the Normans of southern Italy, and, in the East, religious competitors of the Latin Church and dubious allies—sometimes downright enemies—of the Latin Kingdom. This feeling found violent expression in Constantinople itself within less than a year after Manuel's death. The Greeks arose to drive out the thousands of Latins then living there or in the neighborhood. This expulsion was accompanied with bloodshed amounting almost to the proportions of a massacre. The refugees scattered, some of them seeking solace in Tyre, where Archbishop William was then engaged in writing his famous history.

It is difficult not to recognize in the events of the Fourth Crusade which occurred twenty years later some evidence of retaliation for this outrage. The Crusade had started for the Holy Land in 1202 but had been diverted by the Venetians to the capture of Constantinople, their great commercial rival. After great hardships they finally succeeded in capturing the city and sacked it. Their conduct was described later by Innocent III in scathing terms that were fully justified. The Crusaders gave full vent to their passions and wantonly destroyed much of the city. Priceless treasures of art, which they were unable to appreciate, were broken in pieces. The gold and silver and relics were stolen and divided among the hosts. Indescribable orgies accompanied the sack, and the scene of the worst was the great church of St. Sophia. A government was set up under a Latin emperor of Constantinople, but the Latin Empire of Constantinople lasted only a little more than half a century and was always weak. Venice profited greatly because she, by the terms of the agreement, secured "a quarter and a half a quarter" of the Greek Empire, and took as her part mainly islands along the coast. Many of these she long retained. This ill-fated Latin Empire had weakened Constantinople, which never recovered its former strength, and had hurt the cause of the Crusades, partly because the shameless conduct of the leaders in the Fourth Crusade had brought discredit upon the whole movement, and partly because adventurers, in search of booty, were attracted to Constantinople for half a century, and few went to fight in the Holy Land.

It is difficult to sum up the results of the Crusades and the Crusader state in the East. It is very seldom possible, in studying history, to trace influence and borrowings so directly as can be done in the case of the Armenians' debt to the Franks. Usually such matters are illusive, and any references are so indefinite or so slight that the utmost caution is necessary in using them. This was not recognized in the past, and there was a tendency to assert that the advances made in the twelfth and thirteenth centuries were to be attributed to the Crusades, "on the principle of *'post hoc, ergo propter hoc.'* " "So Michelet and Heeren attribute to it all those changes in Western Europe which make its condition in 1300 so marked a contrast to that of two hundred years before. The rise of the French monarchy, the growth of towns all over Europe, the great increase in international trade, the development of the universities, the decline of feudalism, the opening up of Asia, the thirteenth century Renaissance in literature, philosophy, and art—all this was regarded as due to the stir and movement introduced by the Crusades into a sleeping Europe."

Naturally, modern scholars, with a more careful analysis of causes, are sceptical. They know that there was much intercourse with the Saracen before the Crusades; they know that there were other causes for the changes in western Europe; they remember also that there were other channels than the Latin Kingdom through which Muslim influence was penetrating western civilization—the centers of learning in Spain, the polyglot kingdom of the Normans in the South of Italy. Seignobos sums up his statement: "The Crusades undoubtedly had a general effect upon the Christian societies; but for all of these effects there were more active and more positive causes in the people of the West."

Barker and Passant, writing later, while equally critical, recognize certain results which may be attributed to the Crusades. The former states, "Colonization, trade, geography—these then are three things closely connected with the history of the Crusades. The development of the art of war and the growth of a systematic taxation are two debts which medieval Europe also owed to the Crusades. . . . The papacy, on the other hand, had grown as a result of the Crusades. . . . While a new spirit which compares and tolerates thus sprang from the Crusades, the large sphere of new knowledge and experience which they gave brought new material at once for scientific thought and poetic imagination. Not only was geography more studied; the Crusades gave a great impulse to the writing of history. . . . But the new field of poetic literature afforded by the Crusades is still more striking than this development of science. . . . it is all the more significant that the Crusades should have familiarized Europe with new plants, new fruits, new manufactures, new colors, and new fashions in dress. Sugar and maize; lemons and melons; cotton, muslin, and damask; lilac and purple (azure and gules are words derived from the Arabic); the use of powder and of glass mirrors, and even of the rosary itself—these things came to mediaeval Europe from the East and as a result of the Crusades. To this day there are many Arabic words in the vocabulary of the languages of western Europe which are a standing witness of the Crusades—words relating to trade and seafaring, like tariff and corvette, or words for musical instruments, like lute or the Elizabethan word 'naker'."

Passant states that the power of the papacy in the twelfth century culminating in "the position of almost undisputed supremacy occupied by Innocent III" would be difficult of explanation except for the power which the popes had gained as directors of the crusading movement. "The plenary indulgence to crusaders marks an epoch in the development of the system." "Before the crusades papal taxation in the strict sense did not exist." He, too, traces the development of both ecclesiastical and secular taxation through the Crusades. "There can be no question but that the Crusades brought to all three cities in the twelfth century a steady increase of prosperity and wealth." Molinier sums them up in this fashion: "The Crusades finally failed, but they were a turning point in history, the end of the isolation in which lived the states of the West, and the birth of modern Europe. Born of a movement mystic and intensely religious, they contribute to create the laical society of the end of the Middle Ages."

The statements which have been quoted illustrate the divergent points of view and the difficulty of determining the exact influence exerted by the Crusades in so many different fields.

Just as it is necessary to prepare the ground before sowing the seed if the harvest is to be abundant, so western Europe could not have profited if the soil had not been ready to receive the seeds. The advance of the papacy, the growth of the towns, the readiness to accept new ideas, were caused in part by conditions already present in the West. The Crusades hastened the development. Their most important results were the broadening of the intellectual horizon and the enrichment of the West.

CLASSIFIED BIBLIOGRAPHY

of

THE WRITINGS OF D. C. MUNRO

on

THE HISTORY OF THE CRUSADES

THIS bibliography has been prepared for the assistance of those who wish to supplement their reading of the present work with the additional details afforded by the author's other writings on the history of the Crusades. An effort has been made to present here a complete list of his writings on the subject. That the effort has been entirely successful can hardly be expected. He published articles in such a wide range of publications that some undoubtedly have been missed. Furthermore, his more general writings on history and on the Middle Ages which are not included in this list frequently contained illustrative items drawn from the author's special study of the Crusades. That the list is as nearly complete as it is owes much to the help afforded by the chronological list of the author's writings which Mrs. Marion Peabody West prepared for *The Crusades and Other Historical Essays* (F. S. Crofts and Co., 1928), which was presented to D. C. Munro upon his retirement from the presidency of the American Historical Association.

ABBREVIATIONS. — *A.H.R.* — *American Historical Review; Annals—Annals of the American Academy of Political and Social Science; H.T.M.—The History Teacher's Magazine; T. and R.—Translations and Reprints from the original sources of European history published by the Department of History of the University of Pennsylvania.*

BIBLIOGRAPHICAL AND OTHER AIDS FOR THE STUDY OF THE CRUSADES

The key to the vast literature on the history of the Crusades is furnished by the bibliographical sections in *A Guide to the Study of Medieval History.* The revision of this monumental work was undertaken by the Mediaeval Academy of America and was carried out under the immediate direction of Munro.

> Paetow, L. J., *A Guide to the Study of Medieval History,* Rev. ed., 1931 (F. S. Crofts and Co.).

The general reader will find the bibliographical sections in *A Guide to Historical Literature* most helpful. The pertinent sections of this work were prepared under Munro's guidance.

> *A Guide to Historical Literature,* ed. by W. H. Allison, S. F. Fay, A. H. Shearer, and H. R. Shipman (The Macmillan Company, 1931).

Students and teachers in the schools will find the outlines of the subject and his selected bibliographical references especially helpful. These were published in:

A Syllabus of Medieval History, 8th ed. (Longmans, Green & Co., 1919).

"Teaching the Crusades in Secondary Schools," *H. T. M.,* IV.

Brief selected bibliographies on the Crusades appear also in his articles in:

The New International Encyclopedia, 1901; Rev. ed., 1930.

Encyclopedia of the Social Sciences, Vol. IV (The Macmillan Company, 1931).

TRANSLATIONS

Throughout his career as scholar and teacher, Munro encouraged the translation of significant material in foreign languages relating to the Crusades. His chief concern was naturally about the translation of material from the original sources for the benefit of students, but he also encouraged the translation of masterpieces of modern scholarship on this subject. He set the example for both types. His own translations of source material were never mere translations but represented careful scholarly work in selection and annotation as well. This aim he sought also to impart to the many scholars who prepared translations of crusading material with his advice. His own translations include:

Urban and the Crusaders, *T. and R.,* I, No. 2.

Letters of the Crusaders, *T. and R.,* I, No. 4.

The Fourth Crusade, *T. and R.,* III, No. 1.

Several selections in *Medieval Civilization* (joint author with G. C. Sellery), Enlarged ed. (The Century Co., 1914).

ESSAYS AND SPECIAL ARTICLES

Except for the present volume, the author's most extended writings on the Crusades are to be found in his essays and special articles. The essay on the Children's Crusade perhaps affords the best example of the rigorous critical scholarship which was his own ideal and which he sought to impart to his students. In preparation for this study he combed all the extant source material and secondary literature available at the time for every item of positive and probable fact for which there was historical evidence. The resultant article of less than ten pages containing all the established facts affords a startling contrast to the diffuse accounts, often hundreds of pages long, of more romantic writers. The arrangement of this list is according to subject, not the time of his writing.

"Did the Emperor Alexius Ask for Aid at the Council of Piacenza, 1095?" *A. H. R.,* XXVII.

"The Speech of Pope Urban II at Clermont, 1095," *A. H. R.,* XI.

"The Establishment of the Latin Kingdom of Jerusalem," *Sewanee Review,* XXXII, No. 3.

"A Crusader," *Speculum,* VII, No. 3. (Presidential address read at the Seventh Annual Meeting of the Mediaeval Academy of America).

"The High Cost of Living in the Twelfth Century," *Proceedings* of the American Philosophical Society, I, No. 201.

"A Note on the Treatment of Cardiac Disease in the Twelfth Century" (with C. D. Haagensen, M.D.),

Annals of Medical History, New Series, IV, No. 1, pp. 87-90.

"Arabian Medicine as Represented in the Memoirs of Usamah ibn-Munquidh" (with C. D. Haagensen, M.D.), *Annals of Medical History,* New Series, V, pp. 226-35.

"Christian and Infidel in the Holy Land," *International Monthly,* IV, No. 1, 690-704.

"The Renaissance of the Twelfth Century," *Annual Report* of the American Historical Association, I.

"The Children's Crusade," *A. H. R.,* XIX.

"The Popes and the Crusades," *Proceedings* of the American Philosophical Society, LV, No. 5.

"The Western Attitude toward Islam during the Period of the Crusades," *Speculum,* VI, No. 3. (Presidential address read at the sixth annual meeting of the Mediaeval Academy of America.)

Essays on the Crusades (joint author with Prutz and Diehl) (Burlington, Vermont). (Including the article, "Christian and Infidel," previously published in *International Monthly,* 1900).

REVIEWS OF BOOKS ON THE CRUSADES

Though Munro avoided the practice of making a review of a book the occasion for a special essay of his own, it was impossible to avoid the application of his special knowledge of the period. Such material is necessarily fragmentary but nonetheless precious on that account. The following reviews deal with various aspects of the Crusades: Diehl, C., *Byzantine Portraits, Speculum,* II, 350; Schlumberger, G., *Byzance et croisades, A. H. R.,* XXXIII, 904; Dodu, G., *Histoire des institutions monarchiques dans le Royaume Latin de Jerusalem, Annals,* VII, 137; Con-

der, C., *Latin Kingdom of Jerusalem, The Citizen,*
III, 170; Ameer Ali Syed, *A Short History of the
Saracens, Political Science Quarterly,* XIV, 342; Bre-
hier, L., *Croisades, A. H. R.,* XII, 608; Young, G. F.,
East and West through Fifteen Centuries, A. H. R.,
XXII, 139; Röhricht, R., *Erster Kreuzzug, A. H. R.,*
VIII, 163; Chalandon, F., *Alexis Comnene, A. H. R.,*
XVII, 816; Hagenmeyer, H., *Fulcheri Carnotensis,
A. H. R.,* XX, 623; Haskins, C., *Normans in Euro-
pean History, H. T. M.,* VII, 105; Chalandon, F.,
Histoire de la première croisade, A. H. R., XXX,
800; Brehier, L., *Histoire anonyme de la première
croisade, A. H. R.,* XXX, 848; Lees, B., *Anonymi
gesta Francorum, A. H. R.,* XXX, 849; Longnon, J.,
Les François d'Outre Mer, A. H. R., XXXV, 655;
Wright, J. K., *Geographical Lore of the Times of the
Crusades, A. H. R.,* XXX, 801; Moxom, P. S., *From
Jerusalem to Nicæa, Annals,* VII, 302; Miller, W.,
Essays on the Latin Orient, A. H. R., XXVII, 570;
Pears, E., *Destruction of the Greek Empire, A. H. R.,*
IX, 354; Luchaire, A., *Innocent III: la croisade des
Albigeois, A. H. R.,* XI, 365; (same author), *Ques-
tion d'orient, A. H. R.,* XIII, 329; Pissard, H., *Guerre
saint en pays chrétien, A. H. R.,* XVIII, 389; Perry,
F., *St. Louis, Annals,* XIX, 127; Gerland, E., *Latein-
isches Kaiserreich,* Vol. I, *A. H. R.,* XII, 611; Pappa-
dopoulos, J. B., *Theodore II, Lascaris, A. H. R.,* XIII,
896; Gardner, A., *Lascarids of Nicæa,* A. H. R., XVIII,
572; Fotheringham, J., *Marco Sanudo, A. H. R.,* XXI,
846; *Cambridge Medieval History,* Vol. IV, *A. H. R.,*
XXIX, 749; same, Vol. V, *A. H. R.,* XXXII, 574;

same, Vol. VI, *A. H. R.*, XXXVI, 105; same, Vol. VII, *A. H. R.*, XXXVII, 535.

COMPREHENSIVE SUMMARIES OF THE HISTORY OF THE CRUSADES

Thanks to a variety of demands, we have from Munro's pen a series of comprehensive summaries of the history of the Crusades. These are here listed in the order in which he wrote them: article on Crusades in *New International Encyclopedia* (1901); chapters in *The Middle Ages* (D. Appleton and Company, 1902); chapters in *The Middle Ages* (The Century Co., 1921); chapters in *The Middle Ages,* Rev. ed. (joint author with R. S. Sontag) (The Century Co., 1928); article in revised edition of *New International Encyclopedia* (1930); article in *Encyclopedia of the Social Sciences* (1931).

INDEX

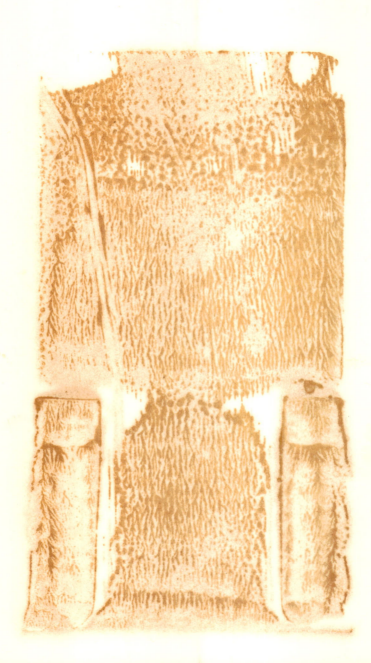